F

SURPRISED BY THE SPIRIT

My wife, Susan, and I are long-time friends of Mary and her husband, Frank. We know Mary to be a person with a passionate heart toward God and a burning desire to see the body of Christ function in all the fruit and gifts of the Holy Spirit. Get ready to be blessed as you read her incredible story of learning to listen and flow with the Holy Spirit.

Dr. Eddie L. Hyatt, Hyatt Int'l Ministries,
Grapevine, TX

I have known Mary Scantlin for over thirty years and have ministered alongside her in retreats. She has powerful insight into the Word of God and delivers it with the Holy Spirit's anointing. As a woman of prayer and with a love for God, Mary has a heart that burns to see the Harvest and see people set free. It is a great honor to recommend *Surprised by the Spirit.*

Carol Torrance, U.S. Regional Director,
Aglow International

SURPRISED BY THE SPIRIT

SPIRIT-LED ENCOUNTERS TO ENCOURAGE FAITH AND HEALING

Mary Scantlin

Worldwide Publishing Group
HOUSTON, TEXAS

www.WorldwidePublishingGroup.com
7710-T Cherry Park Dr., Ste 224   Houston, Texas 77095
713-766-4271

Surprised by the Spirit/Mary Scantlin—1st ed.
ISBN: 978-0-9997837-9-5

Printed in The United States of America

DEDICATION

I dedicate this book to my husband, Frank, whose support and strong encouragement helped make this book a reality.

ACKNOWLEDGMENTS

THANK YOU, God, for drawing me into your saving grace at age 20 and for healing me of fibromyalgia. Your spiritual gifts encourage and help others. The divine encounters reveal your powerful love and intimate knowledge of all our lives. May your love inspire new faith and hunger for Jesus and his spiritual gifts, as seen in these pages.

Frank's steadfast prayers helped toward my healing of fibromyalgia. In time, through the years, I was also healed of back pain and migraines.

May God bless the Houston Episcopal Church of the Redeemer for their healing prayer ministry! I was instantly healed of the migraines there during the years of the Holy Spirit's outpouring.

I am grateful for my husband's strong support through years of the toughest writing process of "making my journal public."

Lastly, I thank all who helped me transform my personal journal into God's book.

CONTENTS

INTRODUCTION

Empowered to Care

ONLY GOD can create a divine encounter. These encounters often reveal how He knows the most intimate details of our daily life! The spiritual encounters I lived through were so stunning that I never wanted to forget one small detail, so I began a journal. Seeing the amazing ways help, grace, and healing were given convinced me that our God is love, as the Bible tells us.

I'm glad I was allowed to "be present" when Father God began touching people in the most incredible and surprising ways! So many have not realized how the powerful, encouraging acts of the Spirit could be sent by God in plain old everyday surroundings.

Life has been extremely tough during the Pandemic, and we can all reach out and encourage one another. God wants to bring such supernatural helps into our everyday life with incredible encounters.

Some worry that we must be special in some way before we can be blessed like this. Others think they have nothing to give. I can assure you that none of that is true! As you establish a time in the Bible, prayer time, and trust in God's grace and faith, you can learn to hear and follow the Lord's bidding into amazing spiritual encounters.

I was shy and introverted. I liked the back of the room! If you feel that way, too, God will help you so that you help others. When the invitations came asking me to speak at Christian gatherings, I thought, *no way!* I felt terrified to stand before a crowd. Nevertheless, this was His call, so I held onto this promise written by Paul to the Believers in Thessalonica:

> *God will make this happen, for he who calls you is faithful.*
> 1 THESSALONIANS 5:23-24, NLT

Jesus said:

> *Most assuredly, I say to you, he who believes in Me, the works that I do he will do also; and greater works than these he will do, because I go to My Father.*
> JOHN 14:12, NKJV

To make this a reality, he sent us the Promise of the Father, the Holy Spirit, who came in great power on Pentecost.

> *"Which," he said, "you have heard from Me, John truly baptized with water, but you shall be baptized with the Holy Spirit not many days from now."*
> ACTS 1:4-5, NKJV

> *Now when the Day of Pentecost came, they were all of one mind and in one place, when suddenly there came a sound from heaven, as of a rushing mighty wind which filled the whole house where they were sitting. Then there appeared divided tongues, as of fire, which sat upon each of them. And they were all filled with the Holy Spirit and began speaking with other tongues, as the Spirit gave them utterance.*
> ACTS 2:1-4, NKJV

At that point, the playing field became level. Peter appealed to the great crowds gathering there to turn away from their old life and thinking, and they would receive forgiveness and a new life. No one was excluded, not even the children. God, in His great love and wisdom, planned this new life to be available to men and women, all classes, ethnicities, and even all children.

The Father designed and portioned out all the spiritual gifts needed for the good of each member of the body of Christ! He is your enabler! So, throughout the centuries, the Spirit of Jesus still baptizes those who give themselves to the Lord. All are empowered to become witnesses of so great a salvation, so rich and so free! Come for the cleansing flow!

Our Lord has rivers for your dry ground. All God's gifts are free, but we must desire them. Earnestly desire them. Then we can give edification, exhortation, and comfort to one another. We each are given a measure of faith. Faith pleases God. How exciting to remember that truth!

Peter reminds us of the importance of personally desiring spiritual gifts. He taught the believers that each one of us has received a gift to help others. We need healing waters to flow to the many who are sick. Let us pray for each other and talk about the healing we've received. This profits everyone who is present, by God's design.

> *Each of you should use whatever gift you have received to serve others, as faithful stewards of God's grace in its various forms.*
> 1 PETER 4:10, NIV

Life gets so complicated at times that we are unsure of what to pray for. How comforting also that we can be sure that when praying in the Spirit's languages, we are praying God's perfect will. This gives us peaceful assurance that our prayers are effective.

CHAPTER 1

Miracles at The Father's House

IN SEPTEMBER 2007, Tom Brand, pastor of The Father's House in the little Texas Hill Country town of San Saba, asked me to minister in a Sunday morning service. He was my brother Dale's pastor, and although I had never met Pastor Tom, Dale had shared many glowing reports about this church, so I was eager to go.

The Father's House

Pastors Tom and Cynthia Brand

I prayed much about the timing for the ministry and the message. Holy Spirit spoke to me often, saying, "You are going with a healing gift for Pastor Tom." I was told to make testimonial copies of the incredible vision and prophecy about Shawn Hannold.

The incredible vision of Shawn's disaster had come to me during worship at Mary Anne Copelin's Bible study. She made you feel loved and welcome. This leader was highly respected by many and well known for her free-flowing spirit-led meetings in Houston. She brought many lost, hurting souls into the Kingdom of God.

I didn't know who I was seeing, but the young man was hospitalized with his right leg up in traction. I sensed he was very seriously injured. Next, I saw something resembling electrical currents moving through the leg. Finally, the Holy Spirit within clearly said, "He will be alright!"

I shared this, but no one in the group responded. At home later that day, though, I got a frantic phone call from Gloria Weeks, who was in the meeting and heard what I shared. I learned this was Gloria's nephew.

She said her brother in Iowa called saying his son Shawn Hannold, was hospitalized with a severe injury. His right leg was up in traction, as the vision showed. These praying, suffering parents were frantic because the doctors were unsure they could save Shawn's leg or his life! They felt certain the leg was full of gangrene.

Hearing this, I thought to myself, *God, they are in Iowa, and we are in Houston! How great are you, LORD!*

Gloria said, "Mary, quick, tell me the vision and prophecy again. They are taking Shawn into surgery, and my brother is waiting for my call."

The Holy Spirit brought hope and comfort in a four-word prophecy, "He will be alright." In fact, that's what happened! Shawn recovered and kept his leg. He owns Shawn's Furniture store in his hometown of Winterset, Iowa. Thank our Lord God Almighty for sending us the Comforter.

The weekend had finally arrived for me to minister in San Saba for Pastor Brand. I made the five-hour drive, but when I pulled up to the hotel, no one was there to greet me! I wondered if I had gotten the wrong date, so I called my brother for assurance that I was in the right place at the right time. He then said he had recently learned that Pastor Tom had suffered a serious bite on one leg, and the prognosis was not good. In fact, the doctors said that if his condition didn't improve right away, he would have to be hospitalized.

After I checked into the hotel, Pastor Tom phoned and told me that his leg was painful and that it was so swollen he might not be able to attend the Sunday services. As I listened, I felt faith rising big in my heart, and I told him the Holy Spirit had long ago said to me that He was sending me with a healing gift for him.

God planned to heal Pastor Tom, and I got to be there! I was beside myself, realizing my calling to intercede and watch the Lord inspire a new faith in us all.

> *For to one is given by the Spirit the word of*
> *wisdom, to another the word of knowledge*
> *by the same Spirit.*
> 1 CORINTHIANS 12:8, KJV

I was so amazed at all the Lord had previously spoken and how He would bring new inspiration and faith to build up the membership of the church. My faith as well! Sunday morning, Pastor and his wife led me into the church office, where I rejoiced as I laid hands on him. God's healing power was flowing for Pastor Tom in an incredible multi-faceted encounter. I praised God in humble astonishment.

That weekend is etched forever in my spirit. God did wondrous things by helping, healing, and strengthening us all with a *Word of Knowledge.* With this gift, you "know" things you have no earthly way of knowing! God urged me to recall how often I'd been given spiritual words of knowledge. Oh, how The Father knows and loves His children! He wanted to heal all manner of sickness. I now had a new awareness of God's desire to touch those needing healing. I was to teach, tell of my own healing of fibromyalgia, and pray for the sick!

There was no medical cure for fibromyalgia. It causes much pain, stiffness, chronic fatigue, depression, anxiety, sleep problems, headaches, and brain fog.

What a miracle when it all was completely gone! I got my life back! I had an instant miracle healing from migraines. But the healing came gradually in my bad knee and the terribly painful back. This tells us not to lose confidence. God loves us, so there must be a purpose for the process of time. If you are suffering, keep going for prayer!

Paul urged the Corinthians brothers and sisters to desire spiritual gifts because spiritual gifts are working together for the benefit of all gathered. Jesus wants us to pray for one another and urges the faithful *to lay hands on the sick, and they shall recover.* (Mark 16:18b NKJV) I really appreciate a doctor's help with medicine. Still, I want prayer by the laying on of hands of believers.

Maybe we've lived in such a way that it caused us sickness. Jesus told one man after healing him to go and sin no more, *lest a worse thing come upon you.* (John 5:14b KJV) God is merciful. He wants to help us, cleanse us, and not condemn us. But healing may very well require lifestyle changes. It's common knowledge that many habits can, in time, affect health.

Maybe it is time to give your heart to Jesus! Make Jesus Lord of all that you are. Pray for cleansing from all wrongdoing. Then, if we truly declare our salvation, we will be filled with peace and a good conscience. In his letter to the people of God, our brother James encourages all to receive healing.

> *Is anyone among you sick? Let them call the elders*
> *of the church to pray over them and anoint them*
> *with oil in the name of the Lord. And the prayer*
> *offered in faith will make the sick person well; the*
> *Lord will raise them up. If they have sinned, they*
> *will be forgiven. Therefore confess your sins to*
> *each other and pray for each other so that you*
> *may be healed. The prayer of a righteous person is*
> *powerful and effective. Elijah was a human being,*
> *even as we are. He prayed earnestly that it would*
> *not rain, and it did not rain on the land for three*
> *and a half years.*
> JAMES 5:14-17, NIV

Clearing Out Obstacles Helps Us
to Receive Healing

Guilt and unforgiveness are two that stand in the way of healing. It's so important to get it right about *forgiveness.* It is not a feeling; it is a decision of our will. Although the *feeling* of forgiveness may happen instantly, it usually occurs gradually.

We must realize that forgiveness does not ignore that a person has hurt us. It acknowledges the truth. Our part is simply to choose to forgive, leaving the rest with the Lord. This frees our faith to operate. Something else to be aware of in receiving healing is the importance of speaking positive words. I read that our bodies respond to our speech center. I experienced this during the final year of my healing in 2005.

I had been sick for eight or nine years and had many moments of real relief, but the pain would return. When I learned to speak God's healing words, I believed one day, that pain would stay gone! So, I spoke God's many promises. By God's grace, I refused to give up my faith.

The power of singing and worship is like medicine for the body and soul. This often plays a significant role in healing. So faith, forgiveness, prayer, and praise are essential in your healing journey. If you are taking medicine, continue to take it until tests show no need. If you have abused your body, make changes by seeking help.

Trust God to strengthen and help you do what is best. Stay in good conscience by repaying debts when possible. All this helps to receive Jesus' peace. Peace is what Jesus left us and is God's will for each of us.

We know that healing grows when we focus on the Bible's teachings. Know what Jesus said and did about sickness, receive the laying on of hands, as James 5:14-16 says. And stay in group fellowship with others who believe in God's healing power. You can be encouraged by their faith as well. (Mark 16:14; Hebrews 6:1-2)

We often see that healing may be instant. Still, more often, it is a process, and at times I become discouraged waiting for the full manifestation. In my case, my wonderful family prayed for me when I was so weak. Their persistence strengthened my faith to press on! Biblical faith believes before it sees the results.

> *Faith is the substance of things hoped for, the*
> *evidence of things not seen.*
> HEBREWS 11:1, KJV

What do we do if we don't experience instant healing? Keep hope. Consider that what seems like NO may simply be a NOT YET. In the meantime, what can we do? We can continue to trust God, receive prayer from trusted believers, and remember to pray God's many promises in faith.

Always know that we are loved by God, our Heavenly Father. So, encourage yourself that the facts show overwhelmingly that He still heals. One of the names by which He revealed Himself in the Old Testament is Jehovah-Rapha, meaning *the God who heals and restores.* (Exodus 15:26 NKJV)

CHAPTER 2

The Early Days

LET ME SHARE the background to show how amazing this was in those early days—and still is today! I was not raised in a Christian home. My mother loved us kids but was divorced and dating, living the single life. My mom and I, plus my two older brothers, moved in with my grandparents in Llano, Texas. Our family never went to church, but when I was around ten, my brother Dale was invited to a revival that was life-changing for him!

There he experienced the love of God enveloping him, and later, at times, his face seemed to shine. Jesus changed him forever. He gave himself to the Lord Jesus, was water baptized, and filled with the Holy Spirit. He radiated joy. We were close, so I knew this was real! He wanted me to attend meetings, but my family didn't allow it. He talked with me often about salvation and prayed for me. He was eight years older than me and soon left for college, found a mate, then moved away. I also married Frank in 1959 in Llano, Texas, my hometown.

From Dale's experience, I knew God was real! I knew my brother was praying for my soul, but I didn't know what to do. We were young and struggled to get by, so I prayed to God that if He allowed Frank to get a job in Houston, I would give my life entirely to Him. When our firstborn, Craig, was a toddler, Frank and I were expecting our second baby. They were my treasure, and I prayed for God's help to raise our babies in a Christian home.

We moved to Houston in 1962, and Frank got a job he was incredibly pleased with. Very soon, I was surprised by weekly visits from nearby Yellowstone Baptist church members, inviting me to church. At times I turned out the lights and didn't answer the door. But oh, how I thank God they didn't give up. They visited me one full year before I finally attended a Sunday service. Though I instantly loved this church and went weekly. I resisted all their calls to be born again and receive salvation.

Late one Saturday night, all the house was tucked in their beds. I was praying in my kitchen about giving my heart and soul to Jesus Christ when the room suddenly filled with the strong, sweet presence of the Lord. At that moment, I gave my life to Him, a heavy weight lifted, and peace filled my whole being.

Overnight, I became a different person. I was filled with joy and told everyone about it! However, I felt sad that my family didn't respond well to my change. They had no interest in a life change. But, by grace, I would go forward praying God would help me raise my babies in a sweet, good life! I found that having a church family was an anchor, especially through tough persecution and ridicule from my loved ones. I often cried to Pastor Bill's wife, Armenta Campbell, for counsel and strength.

My family couldn't know the depth of my conversion and felt they no longer knew me. I cried and asked God for more strength. My answer came when the deacon's wife explained that God was baptizing believers in the mighty Holy Spirit. (Acts 2:1-2)

I learned that a supernatural outpouring of the Holy Spirit touched every denomination. I was excited to have more strength and receive that biblical baptism. Incredibly, my Bible said that the Holy Spirit would pray through me when I felt weak and out of words. I often prayed throughout the day and soon experienced astonishing divine encounters. I also discovered that I would quickly understand how God knows all the details of our lives!

My mother and two brothers visited Houston for a weekend during this time. One morning, my mother was experiencing neck, shoulder, and arm pain. That scared me. We had planned a trip to AstroWorld that day, but I was so worried. She wasn't born again, and she had resisted that for so long that I wondered if God would hear.

I read that God *is patient, not wanting any to perish, but all to come to repentance.* (2 Peter 3:9b, NRSV) Later, everyone went to bed except Mother and me. As we sat and talked, she was still feeling that pain. I was in fear for her life and salvation! Finally, I mustered the courage to ask if I could pray for her. She agreed. I put my hand on her and asked Jesus to heal her. Then, we went back to chatting.

A few minutes later, I heard a loud pop from her body. When I asked what happened, she said her neck popped and no longer hurt. The next morning, she told me that her neck popped again after she went to bed. Although she didn't give her life to the Lord at that time, years later, she did.

My beloved big brother Dale was her caretaker and made sure they prayed nightly! One night he told me that she was visited by the Holy Spirit, and in prayer, a great joy filled her! Soon after, she went to be with the Lord and is forever safe in Jesus.

The Bible taught me God is not willing that any should perish! And He still heals and comforts us.

> *As a mother comforts her child,*
> *so will I comfort you.*
> ISAIAH 66:13, NIV

Do You Need to be Rescued from Guilt's Snare?

If you've ever lived with a sense of guilt, you know it can be devastating. I know from personal experience how scary and miserable that is. It can completely stop us from reaching our God-given destiny if we let it! Imagine the sense of guilt that the apostle Paul lived under! Before his conversion, he murdered scores of godly people. When he met the Lord Jesus in that Damascus Road encounter, he was on his way to murder more!

This encounter of forgiveness and faith caused him to give himself to Jesus. Jesus cleared Paul's guilt and gave him great strength and faith to live his destiny! (Acts 9:1-6, NLT) One sense of guilt can motivate good actions, but when we do what we feel is wrong, the feelings of regret are terrible. In Christ Jesus, we have hope and relief!! But how do you get this relief? John tells us:

> *If we confess our sins, He is faithful and just to*
> *forgive our sins, and to cleanse us*
> *from all unrighteousness.*
> 1 JOHN 1:9, KJV

Often the Holy Spirit shows us how to remedy the situation, but sometimes circumstances prevent it. Other times, even innocent victims of someone else's bad choices can be tormented by a false sense of guilt.

Guilt and its awful grip can burden even a young child. I know this firsthand! 1 John 3:20 teaches us that God is greater than our feelings if we feel guilty. He knows us and understands everything.

When I was very young and thinking I was being helpful, I mistreated a crippled family member. As I grew, I felt extreme guilt that my actions caused him difficulties. I became so filled with guilt and fear that I had nightmares.

For years, I carried that scary feeling of guilt! When I gave my life to Jesus, I wanted to make amends to those I had ever hurt or owed money. Unfortunately, I couldn't fix this devastating situation because the person had passed away.

Then one day during my Bible study, I saw how our Lord Jesus Himself took away the guilt for all who would receive His Lordship over their lives. He became my guilt offering!

> *The chastisement of our peace was upon him; and with his stripes we are healed.*
> ISAIAH 53:5, KJV

I looked at it again and again in disbelief; then, I was filled with peace and so much joy! The sense of guilt left—completely vanished! Though there was no earthly way for me to fix this guilt, Jesus Himself took the burden of it off my shoulders.

The Holy Spirit comforted me! You can pray and ask God's help for you to read and learn in faith that Jesus took all your sin on His own body, so you can live righteously, and through the wounds of the cross, we were healed.

God's word is truth, and you can know this for yourself since many ministries today offer prayers for healing. You may hear about healings five days a week by tuning into CBN, the Christian Broadcasting Network. The healings there come through the spiritual gift of the word of knowledge.

CHAPTER 3

Migraines Healed

AGAIN, IT IS good to understand that we may see an instant miracle. But we often see a process of time cooperating with medical help and therapy. With faith, we offer thanksgiving that we receive. Faith comes by listening to scripture, testimonies, and prayers.

When our youngest child still lived at home, excruciating migraines and the limitations that pain brought me were highly discouraging. But then I heard about the Charismatic Renewal, where healing and other spiritual gifts flowed in every branch of Christianity! None of us had ever seen anything so wonderful.

Protestants worshipped in unity with Catholic nuns and priests. We soon learned that Houston's downtown Episcopal Church of the Redeemer was offering prayers for healing after their regular services. My friends and I were excited to get there every chance we had.

There, we found heavenly worship and a Bible message, and then we were invited to go down to their basement for their laying on of hands and prayers. I had suffered so long and was expecting God to touch me there. One night there, healing came forth instantly in a most powerful way.

Encountering the Power in the Scriptures

Three years after I gave Jesus my life, I was baptized in the Holy Spirit and entered a whole new realm! Scriptures were even more precious, and I felt more sensitive to the nudging of the Holy Spirit. I read scripture daily, and at times, I would open to the same passage multiple times, but not on purpose. I felt I was being directed to look closely at that passage, and there were times this was absolutely the case!

My best friend at this time, Judy Moore, whom I had met at church, was having similar experiences. We were hungry to be in the Lord's Presence, so she dropped off her kindergartener at school five days a week, then came to my home so we could pray and worship together. Time after time, as we talked about the Lord at my breakfast table, the Holy Spirit would suddenly fill both us and the room with a sweet thick awareness of His Presence!

One day, Judy said she kept opening her Bible to Acts 20:9-12, but not on purpose! Here, Paul was meeting with local believers for what would be the last time he would see them on this earth. The meeting went on so long that a young man named Eutychus, who had been sitting in a third-story window, fell asleep, fell to the ground, and died.

> *But Paul went down[ ]...and said, "Do not be alarmed, for his life is in him." Then Paul went upstairs, and after he had broken bread and eaten, he continued to converse with them until dawn; then he left. Meanwhile, they had taken the boy away alive and were not a little comforted.*
> ACTS 20:10-12, NKJV

Soon afterward, Judy went to Colorado to visit her family. While there, she and some family members visited a family living in an upper-floor apartment in their building. Judy's three-year-old son was playing near an open window when he suddenly fell to the cement below.

Panic-stricken, they all ran down and found him bleeding from his nose and mouth. He was alive, but he wasn't responsive. As they rushed him to the ER, they prayed, and Paul's experience in Troas immediately flooded Judy's mind.

She was then filled with great faith, and she knew that her precious son would live and not die. So they hurried him to the ER. By the time they arrived, the bleeding had stopped, and he was regaining consciousness! How blessed we are to have God's powerful Word.

CHAPTER 4

God and the Fax Machine

WHEN I was the administrator and a teacher at Grace School of The Bible in Alief, Texas, I bonded with a young couple, Sheila and David Rogers. David had graduated from both our Basic and Advanced Series of Bible Courses.

During those classes, we experienced the powerful flow of God's gifts as we studied God's word together. A shared experience of the outpouring of the Holy Spirit always has the power to bind us together. But after he graduated from the Advanced course, we went our separate ways and lost touch.

A few years later, David and his little family had remained in my thoughts! I searched everywhere—praying and asking around about him—to no avail. I carried a prayer burden and prayed that God would connect us somehow.

Then, one morning during the Christmas Holiday Season, there was a knock at my door. A telephone repairman said he had been dispatched to fix our fax line. I told him I had no problems and hadn't called a repairman because our fax line was just fine! Then, suddenly, I recognized it was David!

Whopping and hugging him in disbelief, I invited him in, apologizing for my messy appearance as I had been busy baking goodies for our family Christmas. Excitedly I asked, "David! David! What are you doing here? I've searched everywhere for months trying to find you! You have been in my thoughts constantly, and I've prayed to find you!"

He described how he happened to be at my door that morning. He said, "A call came into the office requesting repair service on a fax line. I have the order that stated this address."

I asked, "Didn't you recognize my name?"

"I didn't pay any attention to the name; I was only interested in finding the address."

I responded, "David, I did not call for a repair, and there is nothing wrong with my fax machine or fax line." We just stared at each other, open-eyed, stunned, and marveling at such an incredible divine encounter. My prayers were heard and answered.

Indeed, God's Word tells us that when we call, He hears. In our time of trouble, He says, "I will help you."

> *So do not fear, for I am with you; do not be dismayed,*
> *for I am your God. I will strengthen you and help you;*
> *I will uphold you with my righteous right hand.*
> ISAIAH 41:10, NIV

> *For I am the Lord your God who takes hold of*
> *your right hand and says to you, Do not fear; I*
> *will help you.*
> ISAIAH 41:13, NIV

So, I listened to David share about a difficult spiritual storm in which he had been praying for help and direction. We cried, we talked, and then we prayed. The presence of the Lord was so assuring and strong!

Then David said he had to get to his next appointment. But he asked, "Before I go, is it okay with you if I just check the fax line?"

I laughed and replied, "Sure!"

When he finished, David exclaimed, "There's nothing wrong with the fax line. God did this!"

Like Paul, we can say, "Blessed be the God and Father of our Lord Jesus Christ, the Father of mercies and the God of all consolation." (2 Corinthians 1:3 NKJV) He knows it all and loves us with a steadfast love!

When God Got Mad

One Sunday morning, as I sat in church at Grace Assembly in Alief, Texas, I didn't realize I was about to have an unusual divine encounter. The spirit of Jesus was about to reveal a new glimpse into the fierce love of God. I looked forward to hearing from our visiting evangelist with pleasant expectancy. But my emotions took a big turn, and unbelievably, I felt an intense anger build inside, and I was astonished!

First, I wondered if this had anything to do with the young minister who'd come to bless us. Then, I realized that my focus was being narrowed onto this man's throat area. Anger burned within me, and then there came a calm, knowing it was the Holy anger of the Lord.

Next, I heard the Spirit say, "Satan has oppressed his digestive process. I want it to stop today. Go lay your hand on him and take authority over the enemy in his digestive system. In Jesus' name, command it to stop." He was honorable and apparently, through great hardship, was strengthening the flock, converting souls. God knew and loved him and brought intervention!

This feels like the ferocity of a mother bear whose cub is endangered, I thought.

During altar time, I requested that we all gather around and pray for our guest speaker. I hurried up to be as close as possible and put my hands on him, praying in Jesus' name against his pain and disease *exactly* as I'd been told by the Lord. We dare not take away or add to, a gift of the Holy Spirit.

I held my breath for what would happen next as this was somewhat new to this church. When the furor died down, he said, "I haven't told anyone, but every time after I eat, I endure a lot of pain." Here was my confirmation and his deliverance. What a wonder. We have a great High Priest who is moved with all our infirmities!

He knows every little thing about us and cares when we hurt. This should remind us to go often to sit with him quietly, asking and receiving His help and comfort for ourselves and others. Does Jesus need some more listeners and servants to carry out his desires? Yes! May we all be listeners and doers of the powerful Word of the Master.

A Mighty Power Expels the Darkness

> *The light keeps shining in the dark, and the darkness has never put it out.*
> JOHN 1:5, CEV

How awesome it is to flow with the Holy Spirit to help others. I recall an extraordinary encounter during Halloween when I was in a pinch to get my hair done, but my regular salon was full. So I went to one I had never used and soon knew God's mighty love was reaching for the owner! I was the only client there.

The owner shared some things about her family. As she spoke, I was aware of a strong flow of the spiritual gift of discerning of spirits which revealed more about the family situation. Witchcraft was being practiced, and I urged her to call on God's help.

Although this woman was a stranger to me, she was no stranger to God! He loved her, and He cared for her well-being. In this world, the dark spirits of anti-Christ are what the Bible calls "unclean" spirits. They often masquerade as good spirits, but The Holy Spirit reveals dark activity. She said what I saw was correct, and she sometimes felt uneasy.

At that admission, I shared that Jesus said in John 10:10 that the devil comes only to steal, kill, and destroy. Jesus said He came to destroy those wicked works and give us abundant life! The activity of these spirits often seems harmless, but they can soon show a dangerous side. Jesus's followers can resist in the all-powerful name of Jesus.

We can completely close that door with God's living Word and the power of Jesus' name. We read about all this dark activity in Leviticus 20 in the Old Testament and Galatians 5:19-21 in the New Testament.

I urged her to give herself to Jesus and then learn His teachings. I told her we could pray against this activity. She cried and asked how it was that I knew so much about the Bible. I explained I was called to serve God, and it came from years of studying the Scriptures. I told her I would bring her scriptures to reinforce all we discussed. Back home again, I went to my office and did extensive research to find the scriptures I promised her.

These would give her the knowledge and the faith to change what was negatively affecting her life. I dropped them off the very next day at her salon.

Tears and Comfort Flow at the Cleaners

It was Saturday. I was knee-deep in chores, wearing worn-out jeans, and my hair a ragged mess. As I worked, a nagging thought kept growing louder! I promised my friend Donna that I would give her a testimony tape she wanted to hear, and I could drop it off at her work one day. Now my thoughts were being interrupted as I kept hearing, "Go now!" God meant right now. Yes, sir!

Donna worked nearby at a dry cleaner. I would go but get out quickly! She wasn't there when I walked in, but there was a long line of people. I got in line to ask when Donna would next be there. I was self-conscious, but as I waited in line, I began to feel the Lord's sweet presence, and I thought, *Lord! This is the dry cleaners!* The loving Presence persisted. Knowing it was the Holy Spirit, I asked, "Lord, what do you want?"

He said, "Pray for the woman at the cash register for her son."

Standing in line, I imagined asking to pray for her son, and she would say, "I don't have a son." But I decided a long time ago that whenever I heard the Lord, I would do my best, with the Holy Spirit's help, to obey. The greatest treasure in my life has been my friendship with Jesus! And He tells us what that involves. *You are my friend when you do the things I ask of you.* (John 15:14 NLT para)

As I pondered my situation, my attention was drawn to a teenage girl who came from the back room. I walked over to her and asked if that was her mother at the cash register. She nodded that it was, so I asked if she had a brother, and again she nodded. I then spoke to her in what I thought was a hushed voice, explaining that I felt the love of God prompting me to pray for the cashier's son. The mom heard, and tears welled up in her eyes.

Finally, the last customer left, but a taxi drove up. A very tall man got out and came in. I learned he was the woman's husband and a minister. I assured myself, thinking, *Ah! These are people of prayer.*

So, now I had the mom, dad, and young daughter gathered around me. I simply explained and began praying for their son.

I learned they were, in fact, deeply concerned about the boy. As we clasped hands to pray, my prayer was led by the Holy Spirit. God's awesome purpose and plan were fulfilled! Oh, how I look forward to greeting them again in a place called Heaven.

Paul wrote that God Almighty is a father of mercies and comfort. That day peace and comfort filled the tiny cleaners. This family was assured of several important things: A very personal God heard the prayers of this family, and He would help their son's situation. He wanted to comfort and strengthen their faith. They were also coming into a deeper spiritual understanding of the Holy Spirit's role in prayer.

Jesus said the Holy Spirit is the Promise of the Father, the Comforter. If you long to hear, pray to receive the baptism in Holy Spirit. It's important to read Acts, Chapters 1-2, 8, and 19:1-7. Jesus taught specifics of the Spirit in John, Chapters 14 and 16. You can be sure the Spirit will do what Jesus promised He would when we open our hearts and surrender all. This becomes so real as we let Him lead us. He will say nothing contrary to the scriptures.

> *As one whom his mother comforts,*
> *so I will comfort you.*
> ISAIAH 66:13,TLV

> *Blessed be the God and Father of our Lord Jesus*
> *Christ, the Father of mercies and*
> *God of all comfort.*
> 2 CORINTHIANS 1:3, NKJV

> *But the Comforter, which is the Holy Spirit, whom*
> *the Father will send in my name,*
> *he shall teach you all things.*
> JOHN 14:26A, ASV

Make a quiet place for prayer. Sit with the LORD and listen too. Open the Bible and take a pencil and paper to jot down meaningful thoughts. Then, as time passes, all who learn to be led by the Lord will rejoice!

I will never forget the sweet presence or how the Lord uplifted His children, including me, that Saturday morning!

God's Needle in the Haystack
at the Houston Galleria

Computers provide us with an amazing amount of knowledge. Still, God's treasure chest of knowledge far surpasses all the data on all the computers in the world. He knows our thoughts and all the details of our daily life. He cares when we need encouragement and taught me that, in of all places, at the Galleria!

I had been praying for the Lord's help to balance family responsibilities, so I could also be involved in spiritual ministry. Frank had a new small business where I did everything from payroll to driving the delivery truck. Beyond that, my first love was raising our three children. I was busy! Yet, living with an impossible call to ministry.

One particular day, God called me to step forward in the work of ministry in the body of Christ. I took the first step by reaching out to our pastor, explaining that I had felt a call to serve God for years and felt it was time to begin.

I wanted to visit any in the congregation who needed encouragement, and the Pastor felt good about that. But I prayed, "Dear Lord, please, furnish the time!" Soon, I was ready to leave for work when Frank called, saying he needed me to go to the Houston Galleria for him.

I felt crushed because I had felt such a strong inner leading to visit Barbara, a woman I had just met at church. The pastor had told me that she worked at Sharpstown Plaza, just off I-69, which was on my way.

But now, I must go out to The Galleria instead. I was so discouraged now and doubted that I heard God or truly had a valid call.

Parking at one of the multiple entrances to the Galleria, I walked in and investigated the first store to my right. And there stood Barbara! Even though I had the wrong direction that day, God was in control. It felt like I had found a needle in a haystack. What a wonderful God He is!

"Barbara, what are you doing here?" I blurted out.

She said, "I got transferred! Today is my first day here."

I was stunned, knowing there were at least 400 stores in the Galleria, plus eateries and hotels. I thought, *Dear Lord, you are incredible! I had not known that encouragement is so very important to you! You knew where Barbara was and made sure I got there, too.*

Incredibly and miraculously, I now stood face-to-face with Barbara. I was supernaturally guided there by God speaking to my husband that morning. All of this so that I could obey the leading to encourage a soul He loved.

I recalled that Jesus said:

> *Those who accept my words and obey them are the ones who love me. Because they love me, my father will love them. I will love them and reveal myself to them.*
> JOHN 14:21, NLT

Our Lord revealed Himself so unexpectedly and spectacularly to me that day. I feel awe and such deep quietness in my soul after I see something like this.

Yes, there really is a true God. He certainly revealed Himself spectacularly. He understands where you are and exactly what you are doing here.

Do you know why you are here? You may want to ask yourself and God what you are doing here.

In the meantime, remember that Barnabas' name means *"encouragement."* Our Bible tells us that if we have the gift of encouragement, we should begin praying about it and faithfully listening for the Holy Spirit's leading.

CHAPTER 5

Healing Assignments

THE BIBLE teaches us that God wants us well. In the Bible books of Matthew, Mark, Luke, and John, we read about how Jesus had great compassion for the sick.

> *Jesus went about all the cities and villages, teaching in their synagogues, preaching the gospel of the kingdom, and healing every sickness and every disease among the people.*
> MATTHEW 9:35, NKJV

When I was baptized in the Holy Spirit, I prayed for the gifts to be active as I reached out to others, especially the word of knowledge with gifts of intervention. I learned that using Jesus' name along with faith in the Scriptures is the biblical way to proceed, so I persevered. I'm a witness that healing may be instant or progressive. Either way, it was certain that God still heals us: body, soul, and spirit.

The Book of Acts tells us:

> *...how God anointed Jesus of Nazareth with the Holy Spirit and with power, who went about doing good and healing all who were oppressed by the devil, for God was with Him.*
> ACTS 10:38, NKJV

Jesus is Emmanuel, *God with us*. (Matthew 1:23)

It's good to be persistent while studying the gifts of faith, healing, and spiritual gifts. The dedicated student will gain faith. I took my study material on vacation with me so I could learn and build my faith. I also studied those in healing ministry, like Francis MacNutt (1925-2020), a former Roman Catholic priest, and his wife Judith Sewell MacNutt (b. 1948), a former psychotherapist.

This couple shared not only their successes, but they were humble, sharing times when healing wasn't seen. They prayed about what to do. They saw that fewer people were healed in the bigger meetings. But in the smaller gatherings like retreats, more time was available to give to each person.

They determined that the average individual needed a more extended prayer time of about 20 minutes to see a difference. They wanted to facilitate healing in both the soul and the physical realms. Don't we all need this in our own lives?

During that time, many were drawn to investigate their model for healing prayer. It was different from anything else we had studied. They kept reporting greater help and relief for seekers when they gave at least 20 minutes time to each person.

They called on the name of Jesus, used references to scriptures, and heavily relied on the Holy Spirit's guidance and insight through the spiritual gifts. They rejoiced as they saw more relief, encouragement, and healing for body, soul, and spirit. Any relief is welcome. Their ministry center is still busily ministering prayer today.

By about 2012, I was invited to introduce this ministry approach to local *Houston Texas Aglow International* leaders. Seeing God heal people more often happened as a process, but at times it occurred instantly.

Most healings will take a process of time, and I noted that the Bible tells us that some were healed "as they went." I've been blessed over many years to have seen people instantly healed of fever, a curvature of the spine, stomach pain, and knee pain. And amazingly, the right side paralysis was healed in a few moments.

I love to meditate on and quote Psalm 103 out loud to myself. This is worship for the Lord's wondrous love and help. If you are unfamiliar with the gift of the Book of Psalms, I heartily recommend that you begin reading it. Read a portion of Psalm 103 next.

> *Bless the Lord, O my soul; And all that is within me, bless His holy name! Bless the Lord, O my soul, and forget not all His benefits: Who forgives all your iniquities, who heals all your diseases, who redeems your life from destruction, who crowns you with lovingkindness and tender mercies, who satisfies your mouth with good things, so that your youth is renewed like the eagle's.*
> PSALM 103:1-5, NKJV

When God Shows the Future

During a time of group prayer in our home, I was shown a vision of a couple with their suitcases fully packed. Their daughter was part of our prayer group. I saw a quick move that would be unsettling to family members, but I heard the Holy Spirit say, "This will be a good thing."

We later found out that their company was transferring them to another state. The Comforter was seeking to comfort them by our telling them He had said, "This will be a good thing." Jesus said:

> *When the Spirit of truth comes, he will guide you into all truth. He will not speak on his own but will tell you what he has heard. He will tell you about the future.... The Spirit will tell you whatever he receives from me.*
> JOHN 16:13, NLT

Yes, there are times when it helps to know the future, but God forbids us who are His to seek the future by witchcraft, tarot cards, fortunetelling, tea leaves, and horoscopes. Early on in my Christian walk, I felt to ask for the gift of the word of knowledge. I still experience powerful ways the Lord uses this to bring comfort and help to the hurt, like how the Spirit's gift of knowledge comforted and reassured this family facing a challenge.

What if we see no gift working in our challenging situation? The devil comes to kill, steal, and destroy, but God, in love and perfect wisdom, only does wondrous things! We can continue to do what we know is right and good. The Great Shepherd still leads us. Psalm 23 tells us so.

According to Jesus' description of the Holy Spirit's role (John 16:13-15), we know there are times He wants us to know the future, sometimes by an inner witness, and other times by the ministry of the gifts of the Spirit. (John 14, 15, 16; Romans 8:26-27) Or by visions and dreams, by making a Scripture "come alive," or through an anointed meeting or Bible teacher.

In His wisdom and love, the Lord knows what we need to know. So if you are in a group that acknowledges these things, you can be blessed with a specific word, the word of knowledge, prophecy, faith, help toward healing, or gifts of encouragement. We always need our Bible and our personal quiet time with the LORD. Prayer and worship help us to walk by faith and trust Him in times of need.

Paul said a spiritual gift is given to each of us so we can help each other. (1 Corinthians 12:7, NLT)

Do you ever need help? Of course. We all do. That is why we are commanded to be filled with the Spirit and to desire spiritual gifts. When God wants to use us in a Spiritual Gift, we can be drawn to particular scripture; or hear *a persistent inner voice* inside our spirit. It may be a slight nudge. Regardless of how and when, we can obey in love and compassion, as Jesus did.

CHAPTER 6

God-Given Dream Brings Assurance and Healing

I LED A women's group for our church that was so blessed by the Lord. The Bible teaching, the flow of the gifts, and the sweetness of the fellowship were comforting. I felt close to these women. Many had young children, and I knew their struggles and understood their battles because I had already been through them myself.

God made it very real to me at this time that *He is the great High Priest, who is touched with all the feelings of our infirmities.* (Hebrews 4:15 para.) In a dream, He helped me grasp this in a new way.

I felt close to one mother with a sickly child whom we supported in prayer. Growing up, we rarely went to a doctor because money was tight. For this mother, money was also tight.

One night I dreamed about a massively bruised and feverish injured thigh. Undoubtedly, whoever had been injured like this had extreme pain. The next morning after awakening, I felt led to pray for whoever was in such pain.

Later when everyone arrived for our banquet and was seated, I happened to be sitting beside the young woman with whom I had felt a special closeness. Before long, she said, "Mary, could you follow me to the ladies' room? I want to talk to you."

Once inside the ladies' room, she raised her skirt and showed me her leg. It was exactly what I had seen in my dream, and she was close to tears. She explained that she had stumbled and fallen on the corner of their raised patio. But, unfortunately, money was tight, as with so many young couples, so she hadn't gone to the doctor.

This was a heartrending sight. Yet, joy and faith rose in me because I knew Jesus was with us and would touch her. Filled with joy and compassion, I told her how the Spirit had already shown this to me and that I had been praying for her healing. The relief on her sweet face spoke volumes!

We returned to the banquet, filled with relief, comfort, and awe in our hearts for God. We are all thankful for our doctors, but this encounter could never have happened through treatment in a doctor's office.

Today is Bryan's Birthday

I heard the Holy Spirit say, "Today is Bryan's birthday." It took me by surprise! Bryan was a friend, but I didn't know his birthday. What I did know was that he needed to be comforted because his dad had recently passed away.

As I paid attention to the Holy Spirit, He assured me that Bryan's Dad was safe with Jesus, and my assignment was to comfort him with this fact. So, I called him and explained how the Lord had spoken to me about this being his birthday. That ministered to him and gave him encouragement about his dad's eternal state.

I quickly put together a special *Happy Birthday* package for Bryan. I wanted this gift to testify to God, being our *Abba Father*, as Jesus showed us in Mark 14:36. Seeing the Holy Spirit's gifts at work in daily life has strengthened me! He empowers us by His Spirit to see and hear what He would have us do for Him.

The Necklace

Frank and I were on a cruise in Hungary, and a very nice Bulgarian woman serviced our cabin. One day, she noticed my cross necklace and remarked how much she liked it. The Lord prompted me to use this to share with her how Jesus loved her and gave himself for her salvation. That night I wrote out a Scripture and a prayer. I left it where she would find it when she came to clean our room. The next morning, she thanked me and said that it was so beautiful.

She then explained that she read many kinds of books but not the Bible. She said nothing she had ever read affected her like what I had copied for her. "It just hit me, but in a good way," she said.

It was such a blessing, and she wanted to know more. She went on about her business, but I prayed for her before Frank and I went ashore that day. Later, I wrote four pages of Bible verses that majored on what Jesus did for us and how the Holy Spirit was sent to us. Then we parted ways. God will complete His good work.

The Little Girl on the Bike

At The Encourager Church service some years back, the leaders began the service by asking us to learn more about the heart of God by seeking Him in a quiet prayer time. We find value in quieting our spirit after a full and hectic day to discover again how wonderful our God is.

At this time, in my mind I saw a picture of a lighthouse whose light was unusually bright. It seemed exceptionally bright because the night was very dark. And then, in my spirit, I heard the words, "Brightly beams our Father's mercy."

It is because He cares that His Spirit lights our pathway, especially in times of danger, darkness, and need.

> *Your word is a lamp to guide my feet and a light*
> *for my path.*
> PSALM 119:105, NLT

Seeing the lighthouse in my mind's eye caused me to immediately remember a dark day in my life a few years back. But because God shined His light on my path, He saved four of us from injury. To further explain, my plan had been to meet my friend, Diana Quisenberry, and drive together to a conference.

As I was about to leave my house, an ominous, dark feeling brought me to my knees, and I asked, "Lord, what is this? What's wrong?"

I kept praying in the Spirit in my prayer language, and 1 Corinthians 14:15 poured through me like a flash flood. All the while, Diana was waiting patiently for me, but because of the delay, she phoned, wondering if I would still pick her up. I explained the situation and let her know something was wrong. I didn't know exactly what! She tried to comfort me, and she urged me to come on.

I was young in the Lord, still learning much about Him and His ways. We talked and prayed some more, and finally, I gathered my daughter and picked up my precious bundle—my third child, who was a few months old—and I was on my way.

About halfway to her place, I came upon a big field where children were playing ball. It was a busy spot, with a big crowd and many cars and pickups on both sides of the road.

Suddenly, a horrific vision flashed across my mind. It was a picture of a little girl to my right on a bicycle, darting out right in front of my car. And in the vision, I slammed on my brakes. Immediately, a little girl on a bike *really did* dart out right in front of my car! I hit her but thank God, the impact was so minor that her bike barely turned over, and she fell quite gently to the ground.

Inside the car, my infant son tumbled onto the floor. This was before the days of car seats. I gathered and held him close, thanking the Lord that he was safe and that my daughter was not hurt. As for me, I was rejoicing that because of the strong Spirit-led prayer and the vision God had given me, I was able to hit the brakes just in time!

In this near tragedy, the Spirit of Truth knew what was coming, got my attention, and poured intercession through me because I didn't know how to pray.

Jesus Reveals This Spirit of Truth

I will pray the Father, and He will give you another Helper, that He may abide with you forever—the Spirit of truth, whom the world cannot receive, because it neither sees Him nor knows Him; but you know Him, for He dwells with

> *you and will be in you. I will not leave you*
> *orphans; I will come to you.*
> JOHN 14:16-18, NKJV

The Spirit of Truth is the Holy Spirit, our Helper. He Himself prays for us because we don't always know how to pray. Paul writes:

> *The Spirit also helps in our weaknesses. For we do*
> *not know what we should pray for as we ought,*
> *but the Spirit Himself makes intercession for us*
> *with groanings which cannot be uttered "***in***
> ***articulate language.***"
> ROMANS 8:26, NKJV (EMPHASIS ADDED)

In the Old Testament, the Holy Spirit came upon certain people at special times for specific reasons. But when the Day of Pentecost arrived, the Holy Spirit came to *live in* all the followers of Jesus so they—and we—would be empowered to carry out His work. (Mark 1:8; Acts 2)

On that special day, He came to stay. He announced the event in the Upper Room (where the disciples were staying) by a mighty, rushing wind and by appearing as tongues of fire on the heads of those gathered for prayer. They were so excited that they went out to the streets to tell the multitude what had happened, and they spoke to them by the empowering of the Spirit in languages they had not learned. In other words, they had received the divine ability to speak in tongues.

How blessed we are! As followers of the Lord Jesus, we have the scriptures, the gifts of the Holy Spirit, and His indwelling presence. All of this is ours to claim, to receive! In the same way that we must claim an earthly, inherited gift of money for it to be ours, we must claim the inheritance God has provided.

Is just believing enough? The Bible says the devils believe, yet their destiny is not heaven! (James 2:19) So, to be eligible for your inheritance, you must give yourself wholly to Jesus so that Jesus becomes not only your personal Savior but also the Lord of your life. We can become *doers of the word.* (James 1:22)

God's Light shines brightest in darkness! Jesus is the Light of the World, and He promised:

> *I have come as a light to shine in this dark world so that all who put their trust in me will no longer remain in the dark.*
> JOHN 12:46, NLT

Despite the trials that we all go through. (Isaiah 50:10) God promises never to leave us nor forsake us. (Hebrews 13:5-6) We can trust Him completely.

Sometimes we don't have any foreknowledge of impending trouble, and sometimes we don't experience deliverance from trouble and trials—but we find we are strengthened as we walk it out with Him. Assuredly, in such times it is important to expect help from the LORD.

There is a proven benefit when we sing. There is also a benefit in taking Paul's advice that we are to give thanks, not *for* all things, but *in* all things. I found peace in what the great Prophet Isaiah says:

> *Who among you fears the Lord? Who obeys the voice of His Servant? Who walks in darkness? And has no light? Let him trust in the name of the Lord. And rely upon his God.*
> ISAIAH 50:10, NKJV

The Red Lobster Lady

One day in prayer, I heard myself repeating the word "Zapata." I prayed this word several times over the next two weeks. Then one night, my husband and I went to eat dinner at Red Lobster. While there, I found myself staring at a woman who was boldly staring back at me! We finally went to the lady's room, where she blurted out, "Oh, I know this is God!" And I was electrified to learn that her last name was Zapata.

This is how and why the Holy Spirit prays through us. We don't know how to pray that we might meet a hungry, longing soul named Zapata. I learned she was Catholic, and her strongest desire was to study the Bible. Here I stood, a protestant who was teaching Bible to

Catholic and Methodist women in Alief, Texas. God does wondrous things!

Marti Whalen, a dear friend and neighbor, had opened her home for the Bible study. So I told my new friend about our group and gave her Bible study workbooks. How amazing was Jesus' strategy to satisfy a hungry soul.

CHAPTER 7

Learning the Obedience of Faith

MY CHILDREN and I found a new church plant meeting in the Sharpstown home of a couple who were dedicated teachers. This was during God's incredible outpouring of the Spirit on all faiths. The revival began approximately in the early '60s and became widespread through the mainline denominations. We were a small group of devoted believers from different Christian backgrounds who experienced the baptism in the Spirit as the New Testament describes.

I was so glad that my children could experience a strong spiritual atmosphere! We were all hungry for more of God, his Word, and the Holy Spirit's Spiritual gifts for the benefit of the entire Body of Christ.

We wanted to bring souls into the joy of salvation. Therefore, we studied God's Word in our meetings while waiting for the Holy Spirit's flowing gifts. Peter taught that this flowing group ministry was significant and exhorted the church, saying:

> *As each one has received a gift, minister it to one another, as good stewards of the manifold grace of God.*
> 1 PETER 4:10, NKJV

To make it even better, our leader's wife always had a delicious freshly baked cake on the counter waiting for us. We loved her.

One Sunday morning in worship, I kept staring at our leader's wife because I saw a little white cloud on her abdomen. It was not like something I could reach out and touch, but it seemed to be a gift within me to see this vision on her abdomen. I kept praying until the spiritual gift of the word of knowledge revealed a bad ovary. I was impressed to pray for healing by laying hands on that specific area. This woman was so strong in faith, and I didn't doubt that healing could happen.

That Sunday evening would be our next meeting. We learned to be open to spiritual gifts and knew to test every leading according to the character of God and the Bible. This is how we "tested the spirits." Visions were biblical, and I knew that Jesus' command was to lay hands on the sick, and they would recover. All this activity passed the test!

The biggest problem was that I was sure that she had no ovaries. Because at an earlier meeting, she shared about having female surgery where they removed everything.

I was younger than most there and distressed at being told to lay my hand on her to heal an ovary when there was no ovary. I found the courage to pray for our leader's wife and went to put my hand on her shoulder. I heard a big "No," and then Holy Spirit said, "Now lay your hand where the problem is and pray healing for this ovary in Jesus' name."

Winnie gladly welcomed the prayer. The Lord planned to heal, but I gathered the nerve to ask, "Didn't you tell me that you had surgery for female problems, and everything was removed years back?"

She said, "Yes, that's true. But they left the one ovary and said it would probably be good for about ten years before it must be removed."

When she said it had been ten years, we were stunned and praised the Lord. Dear Lord Jesus, how compassionate you are to heal us.

One night, as I dressed to go to the meeting, I realized my oldest son, who was around twelve years old, had become sick and limp with a fever.

No meeting tonight, I thought. Instead, I would prepare juice, tend to, and comfort my son.

But I began to feel great confidence to take him to the meeting. I recalled 2 Corinthians, where it says:

> *Blessed be the God and Father of our Lord Jesus*
> *Christ, the Father of mercies and the*
> *God of all comfort.*
> 2 CORINTHIANS 1:3, NKJV

So I bundled him up, praying for his comfort and touch from the Lord. Ten minutes after we arrived and all prayed, he was no longer flush nor limp. He was well and played with the other children. We were full of joy and holy awe! Lord, you truly still heal today.

He Heals the Brokenhearted

After our home group was dissolved, we joined the nearby Grace Church. As I sat in our Sunday morning service, I became deeply concerned for a godly woman who was brokenhearted and consumed by profound grief. She had discovered that her husband was leaving her and their three children to live with a woman he worked with, who was expecting their child. My heart ached for her.

At the time, I was head of our Women's Ministries Department and knew that our women were worried for her and trusting God for her deep sorrow. Psalm 147:3 tells us more about the compassion of our Lord.

> *He heals the brokenhearted and binds up their*
> *wounds.*
> PSALMS 147:3,NKJV

I was lost in my concerns for her through the worship and sermon. It was now time to invite those in need to come forward to receive prayer.

This lady went forward, and I saw someone praying with her. I felt love and compassion toward her. But not wanting to interrupt what was happening, I simply went down and stood close to show my support.

I was going to touch her shoulder lightly to let her know I was there. But as I reached out, a strong, invisible force took hold and drew my hand to a specific spot between her shoulders. Incredibly, it felt like my hands were melting into her body and being held there.

Also, a current flowed from my hands as I'd never experienced before. What a wondrous moment! Jesus was ministering by His Spirit. The Comforter had come! Jesus knew her and knew exactly what she needed.

When the prayer ministry ended, I still felt glued to her and leaned my head around to ask if she knew why my hands should be in a specific spot between her shoulders.

Through her tears, she said, "Oh, I wasn't even going to come to church today. I failed the Lord when my husband came to the house to get some things. I was so hurt that I lost control and flew at him in a rage. I was hitting him and threw something out between my shoulders right where your hand is now. I felt so condemned I could not ask my pain to be healed."

I continued feeling the power flow of the Holy Spirit's healing going into her body, so I asked if she could tell me what she was feeling at that moment.

She broke down and said, "All the pain is leaving!"

I marvel in humility that I was the vessel used to pour His powerful love and medicine into the depths of this woman's pain and suffering. I had never felt the tangible anointing of the Holy Spirit manifest so strongly within my own body.

The two of us had experienced the spiritual gift of healing. For weeks afterward, I lay in bed thinking how God had come to my friend, who was hurting so badly. And by His Holy Spirit, how He had brought healing, comfort, and strength when she could not go to Him herself.

Paul wrote:

> *Blessed be God, even the Father of our Lord Jesus Christ, the Father of mercies, and the God of all comfort, who comforts us in all our tribulation, that we may be able to comfort them which are in any trouble, by the comfort wherewith we ourselves are comforted of God.*
> 2 CORINTHIANS 1:3-4, KJV

About six months later, while walking across my kitchen, I heard the Holy Spirit ask, "Do you remember the woman who was so convicted she wasn't going to come to church and wasn't going to ask me to help and heal her?"

I said, "Oh, dear Lord, yes! And I am so thankful I got to be there when You did that! I could never forget such love and forgiving power as I felt that day!"

Then He began a teaching moment with me. At that moment, it occurred to me that He wanted me and all other teachers to be correct in what we taught. I heard the Spirit say, "That is what the scripture means: *If our hearts condemn us, God is greater than our hearts who understand us and knows all things!*" (1 John 3:20)

How marvelous to think about! And you can be sure that means you. So give Him your life today. Indeed, you are dearly loved.

Destination: Life-Changing Coffee Bar

A few years before the financial collapse of 2008, Frank and I were visiting relatives in the Texas Hill Country. We reserved a motel room, expecting a nice breakfast bar and great coffee. But what a disappointment both were!

Then, too, the lighting in our room seemed dim! I grumbled that the owner must be afraid that he couldn't pay the bills. I was in a haughty, grumpy mood!

After we got settled, Frank went out, and I stayed there, feeling even more grumpy, haughty, and impatient. I thought I deserved better conditions than this. But in my prayer time, I saw my attitude as terrible.

So I asked for forgiveness, help to walk in divine love, and the ability to pour out His love to others.

The next thing that happened was totally wild and unexpected. I heard the voice of the Holy Spirit say, "The owner *is* worried about paying the light bill!"

Suddenly, it was as if the curtain of time and space had been pulled back, and I could see what God was seeing about this proprietor, a young man from India. I was being shown his thoughts and troubled emotions.

How God loves the world! I felt that great love reaching for this young man—a person who was *so* different from me and yet no different at all! Heaven had come down. Compassion flooded my being. My orders were to tell this young man that God loved him, knew about his anxious thoughts, and wanted to help him!

Before long, I saw him in the hall and explained that I knew he was very worried about the business. His astonished look and his tear-filled eyes are forever etched on my heart. Astounded, he kept asking how I knew. I told him that Jesus' Holy Spirit told me during my prayer time. What a delight to tell him that Jesus and the Holy Spirit were full of love for him and knew everything about his worries and life.

He had come from India and was working hard to get ahead. When I asked him if he had a Bible, he said, "Yes," and that he had read it all the way through! He asked me again how I knew, and I urged him to read the Book of John, Chapters 14-16.

The next day, he came out as we were loading the car. He mentioned that he and his wife had lost their first baby and were expecting again. I asked if he wanted prayers, and we prayed right there on the sidewalk for a healthy baby.

I assured them again of Jesus' great love and how He speaks to us through His Holy Spirit and the Bible. Then, I gave him a little book explaining how to give himself to the Lord Jesus and what it means to receive his salvation.

Later, my brother Dale visited the young man, thinking of praying for his salvation. But the young man said emphatically, "From the day your sister prayed, I have had Jesus in my heart!"

> *I tell you the truth, anyone who welcomes my messenger is welcoming me, and anyone who welcomes me is welcoming the Father who sent me.*
> JOHN 13:20, NLT

As I thought about this divine encounter, it occurred to me that we may not really appreciate what it means to be saved. The word "salvation" is the English translation of the Greek word "*sozo.*"

The meaning of *sozo* includes "freedom from the power and guilt of sin, physical healing and mental well-being, deliverance, and peace. Having favor with our

God and Father." It is not something that we can create. Only the LORD can save. We are a privileged people!

CHAPTER 8

A Spiritual Leading Overruled Dark Despair

I HIT a place where I really wondered how I could go on as I was so worn down! I knew God loved me but didn't understand why He didn't send relief for my difficult circumstances.

My painful emotions seemed so unbearable. I just wanted to find relief. I began to dwell on those thoughts. One night, I swallowed a bottle of aspirin pills and laid down to end it all, but my thoughts about my three precious children soon overwhelmed me. I could not leave them!

I threw up the aspirins to face life again, albeit feeling angry at God for not coming to my rescue! I couldn't imagine admitting it, but in the recesses of my mind, I decided I would not speak to Him. I would just remain silent.

After the failed suicide attempt, I attended a small church in Stafford, a suburb of Houston. The interim pastor there was incredibly joyful, and I was glad to be part of this church family. This Stafford, Texas, church welcomed the Holy Spirit's spiritual gifts, and the fellowship was always meaningful.

With our two youngest children in tow, I went several times a week. The Word of God and the Holy Spirit's lead helped me through the following week. However, I can never forget one particular day when I felt utterly drained and lonely. I told myself I would go through the motions but no longer listen to or speak to God.

As we settled into our seats, I took special note of a friend's young daughter coming towards me. Suddenly, our eyes locked! The little girl then stood very close to me, and her eyes were cast down. Then, in a strong, sweet voice, she spoke a powerful prophetic word to me, saying, "I love you. Please, don't be mad at Me. Come close to Me. I love you so much. I don't want you to be mad at Me. I love you so much."

I dissolved into a heap of flowing tears on the floor. What a great high priest is our Jesus! What a Savior! What a tender Shepherd. He rescued this wounded lamb!

> *We do not have a high priest who is unable to sympathize with our weaknesses, but we have one who in every respect has been tested as we are, yet without sin. Let us therefore approach the throne of grace with boldness, so that we may receive mercy and find grace to help in time of need.*
> HEBREWS 4:15-16, NRSV

I couldn't wait to find this little girl's mother to share the awesome way she had listened, heard, and obeyed our Lord! May this generation of youth today experience our great High Priest, the God of Peace, who loves the world and gave His son for our eternal salvation.

When my friend's precious little girl finished speaking from God's heart to me, she just walked away and continued with what she had been doing. The children had been taught God's word. She knew about Jesus's Spirit and spiritual gifts. She saw and heard them in action in our little group, so she was confident in obeying the Holy Spirit by prophesying what was given to her.

I was astonished! What a profound impact that experience had on me! I can genuinely say that I never again allowed such hardness to grip my heart. I was never the same after receiving such gracious love prophesied to me through such an innocent child.

How could this be? How could God use a child to help me? To understand all this, we need only look to the coming of the Holy Spirit on the Day of Pentecost.

This Promise is for You

The Day of Pentecost arrived. Who could explain the loud wind, the tongues of fire, and the power?

> *Peter, standing up with the eleven, raised his voice and said to them, "...But this is what was spoken by the prophet Joel: '...In the last days, says God, That I will pour out My Spirit on all flesh. Your sons and your daughters shall prophesy....'"*
> ACTS 2:14-17, NKJV

In the Book of Acts, Chapter 2, Peter lists the activity of the Holy Spirit that would happen in the lives of believers anywhere they gathered because of this outpouring from Heaven.

These spiritual gifts are listed in Romans, Chapter 12, and 1 Corinthians, Chapter 12. These include dreams and visions, spiritual language, and prophecy—Peter said they would be experienced by the young and old, men and women, and people at all levels of society, including men and women servants.

Peter taught the crowds how to receive:

> *Repent and let every one of you be baptized in the name of Jesus Christ for the remission of sins, and you shall receive the gift of the Holy Spirit.*
> *For the promise is to you, your children, and all who are afar off, as many as the Lord our God will call.*
> ACTS 2:38-39, NKJV

This promise is for *whoever* calls on the Name of the Lord. It's not determined by race, age, gender, or class. What an awesome God! He only does wondrous things!

I will never forget how Jesus saved me. It seemed a weight lifted off my very being, and great peace filled me. I will always treasure being baptized in the Holy Spirit and how a whole new bold realm of life becomes ours. We become bold witnesses willing to share God's power, mercy, and grace. We believe *that through God, we will do valiantly, for it is He who shall tread down our enemies.* (Psalm 60:12 NKJV)

God's Mighty Power for Sister Martin

God's mighty power is at work within those who believe in Jesus! What does this mean? What does it look like? Paul says it is both mighty and effective!

> *Now all glory to God, who is able, through his mighty power at work within us, to accomplish infinitely more than we might ask or think.*
> EPHESIANS 3:20, NLT

I experienced the mighty working of His Spirit some time ago when a good friend, Diana Quisenberry, invited me to speak to the women's group at her church. I had not been to this church before. During prayer and ministry time, my attention kept being drawn to a particular woman. I learned later that she was called Sister Martin. I strongly sensed that she needed prayer, but she didn't respond to the invitation.

Everything in me wanted to pray for her! So, I left the group of those gathered at the front and headed down the aisle to where she was seated. I stood before her and asked, "Don't you need prayer? I feel strongly that you have a need!"

She said, "Yes, I have severe back pain, but I've been prayed for so many times, and nothing has ever happened. So, I just didn't have the faith to go again."

Her faith was weak, but she had gotten herself to the meeting. Her weakness didn't stop Jesus' compassion from being poured out on her. Jesus was reaching for her. He stirred in me the spiritual gift of the word of knowledge to change her life. Help and love replaced her weak faith. This reminded me of how Jesus reached out to Peter when his faith faltered. And Jesus wants to encourage your faith, too. Jesus said:

> *Simon, Simon, listen! Satan has demanded to sift all of you like wheat, but I have prayed for you that your own faith may not fail;*
> *and you, when once you have turned back, strengthen your brothers.*
> LUKE 22:31-32, NRSVUE

In talking with Sister Martin, I learned that the doctors could find no cause for the terrible pain in her back. This happened around the mid-1980s when doctors only had X-rays to diagnose medical problems. So, I explained that God was leading me to pray for her. She agreed.

When I laid my hands on her, the Holy Spirit gave me a word of knowledge for her, and I heard, "The problem is not her back. It's female trouble." So I shared this and prayed then for the specific problem!

A few weeks later, Diane phoned and asked excitedly, "Did you tell Sister Martin that her back pain was caused by a female problem?"

I exclaimed, "Yes, most definitely!"

She explained that when the doctor did exploratory surgery, he discovered a tumor. But it was on the back side of her ovary where no X-ray had been able to show it. The doctor removed it.

Then, Sister Martin's highly unusual quick recovery and release were remarkable. Diane said that turn of events really had the hospital buzzing!

If I were God, I would have totally zapped that tumor! But oh, the love and encouragement she would have missed! He had a much bigger plan in mind. A miracle of physical healing was secondary to the most important things that this woman needed. Like most of us, she needed to feel love and have her faith encouraged. She needed to know God deeply loved her and cared about her faith! In His mercy and compassion, He revealed to me the exact physical problem, and I could hear it inside through the gift of the Holy Spirit's word of knowledge.

Jesus knew how to bring help to Sister Martin. Despite what the enemy tried to convince her of, she found that her many prayers were indeed heard and valued. Jesus knows how to help you also. You can trust His mighty compassion. I investigated Romans 8:28 at my weakest points.

There is hope at your weakest point. Keep company with other believers and investigate the scriptures. Trust His help. In this case, the word of knowledge proved to be a real faith-builder—as are all God's gifts! So, let's obey the Biblical exhortation:

> *Pursue love, and desire spiritual gifts....*
> 1 CORINTHIANS 14:1, NKJV

God has given each one a measure of faith so we can reach for more fruit in our lives.

CHAPTER 9

A Heavenly Basket of Flowers

WHEN I WAS a young mother and the eldest of our three children was a young teenager, I was introduced to Pastor Worthington and his wife at a local Bible study. This couple was humble, strong, and wise, and their group flowed in the Holy Spirit's gifts. How I wanted my life to be more like theirs. They were so calm; it seemed they had a very peaceful life.

I felt so drawn to them that, one day, I found all the shoes needed to get the three children ready and drove across town to be part of the meeting in their little white country church. The presence of the Lord was so strong and sweet. Jesus was honored, and the worship was so rich. The preaching was anointed, and the spiritual gifts were flowing freely. My children and I were loved each week, and I felt so strengthened!

Sometimes we had flowers on the platform, and one Sunday night, the pastor's wife told us a story. She said one hot Sunday morning that she was straightening up after everyone left the building. And as she looked at the flowers, she decided to take them home with her since they would just wilt and die in the heat.

But as she reached for them, she was transported into a very special moment, hearing, "But those are my flowers."

This showed that the small gift of flowers showed love for the Lord and His gathering, and therefore He took pleasure in them. At that moment, she felt wrapped in a blanket of God's love.

As we listened, we were filled with wonder and a sense of awe. God is the Creator of the Universe, and yet, He is so tenderhearted toward each of us, His children. Even the smallest things matter to Him. We can't forget how much the LORD loves His children.

I Will Praise You, O Lord, With My Whole Heart

> *I will tell of all Your marvelous works.*
> PSALM 9:1B, NKJV

Our three kids, Craig, Tammy, and Brent are now grown with their *own* busy lives. Each of them has given us so many great memories. And the grandchildren—each one a blessing—continue to fill our treasure chest with fun little memories. I've come to realize that the little things can be so important.

Little is much when love is in it! And *little is much when God is in it!* We should be aware that, at times, God can direct us to take some seemingly small actions that can change a life. Little becomes much when God is in it.

The Lost Earring

When Tammy was a teenager, at one point, she decided to attend Church of the Southwest, which had a thriving youth group not far from our house. Soon after, I felt directed there. I shared this with the pastor of the church we had been attending, and he gave us his blessing to go.

This move in the early 80s made a difference for me in ways I had not anticipated. For years, I had been sensing a strong call to ministry. While my inner being longed to obey, I had held back because of fear and circumstances. But the time had come! I entirely dedicated myself to God's will to serve. I told our new pastor I wanted to serve somehow.

Soon I was attending the women's ministry business meeting at the church. This was their meeting to elect new leaders. Since I was new in the congregation, I hadn't yet made any friends, so I was stunned when someone nominated me for Women's Ministries President. I was elected! I accepted! But with no previous experience, I had no clue what to do. I took one baby step at a time and was joyfully ready to learn.

Bit by bit, God knit our group together, working mightily among us. His wonderful gifts of healing and His nurturing Presence caused a great love to grow among us. I was deeply touched on my birthday when the group honored me with a joy-filled lunch and a pair of pretty earrings. They were inexpensive, but to me, they were a precious symbol of the women's love and God's approval of those first shaky baby steps.

One day, I realized that one of my cherished earrings had fallen off and was lost. I searched and searched, but it was nowhere to be found. My heart sank, but I didn't give up hope of finding it. I kept praying that it would show up. Several days passed! Then, my son, Brent, came home from school holding my earring. He asked, "Mom, isn't this the earring you've been looking for?"

Well, I screamed. I laughed. And I jumped up and down. I was so happy and so relieved! "Where was it?" I asked.

He said that he and his friends stopped for a treat at the 7-Eleven after school, and he saw it glittering in the parking lot. I was speechless and overcome with a sense of God's love and how much He cared about the little things that matter to us. Almighty God, the Creator of the Universe, is our Father.

Jesus Cards

I've noticed how God uses what we think are little things to accomplish His purposes. An example is what I call

"Jesus Cards" that I make. I pray over them and give out as I feel led. A card can fit in a shirt pocket.

No one has refused to accept one of these cards from me. But one day, a young man, the valet at a small restaurant where I was eating, hesitated!

I looked him in the eye and said, "I know that you love Jesus."

With that, his eyes lit up, and he took the little card. As I left the restaurant, he rushed over to me, saying how glad and thankful he was to have the Jesus Card. His heart was so touched.

On another occasion, I gave one of the cards to my hairdresser, an enthusiastic Christian. When I went for my next appointment, she told me that she was taking the card with her on a trip to attend a family wedding. She said it was such a comfort to her. But when she unpacked and looked for it, she was upset that it was nowhere to be found. She had left it in the pocket of her smock back at the shop, so that was the end of that.

Over a week later, she came to work, reached for one of the hanging smocks, and found the Jesus Card waiting for her. She was so joyful as she told me all the details.

The seemingly little things the Holy Spirit prompts us to do can mean big things in someone's life. We never know exactly how Jesus can use us as we respond to His promptings. But don't you have the desire to serve as Jesus' hands, heart, and voice? I do!

He is still moved by compassion. The great commission details our mission to touch the lives of others. God's love is reaching out for His other lambs.

So, Jesus has told us to bring them to Him, the Good Shepherd. He has told us to be led by the Holy Spirit, the Helper, Comforter and Stand By—to live in Him and to walk through life by the power of His Spirit.

Beloved Grandfather

The Holy Spirit prompted me to give a Jesus card to a young man working on our home. He asked for one for his work partner, which led to us talking for a while. He said that he had Bibles but that he had never read any. As we spoke, the Holy Spirit alerted me that somebody in his family was in a most challenging situation. They were in pain, and it seemed that something life-threatening was happening.

As I shared how God loved him, he told me his greatly beloved grandfather was the one suffering. I prayed and urged him to see that his grandfather receive prayer with the laying on of hands. (Mark 16:18)

At one point, when I prayed in the Holy Spirit for him and his family, He asked if I was speaking French. I said this was the Holy Spirit praying the will of God. He asked how I learned this language. I explained that it was a gift of God from the outpouring of Jesus' Spirit on the day of Pentecost.

I told him that when we are unsure how to pray, then by the Spirit, we are able to pray the very will of God. He let me know he was eager to learn more.

It is so important to know what Jesus said in Luke:

> *So I say to you, ask, and it will be given to you; seek, and you will find; knock, and it will be opened to you.*
> LUKE 11:9, NKJV

I explained and encouraged him to read his Bible, beginning with the Book of John.

He texted me later to say that the prayers of their church were comforting, and that his beloved grandfather had indeed passed and was with the Lord. He shared, too, that surprisingly and thankfully, it was as if he had already made peace with it all. It was as if the Lord had comforted him through our prayers.

We must remember that God is Spirit (John 4:24). The scriptures remind us to walk in God's Holy Spirit and know His word in scripture because we live in a dark world where dark spirits are active.

It seems that many in the Body of Christ may not fully realize this. But God has created us as spirit, soul, and body. It has been correctly said that we are spirit, have a soul (mind, will, and emotions), and live in a physical body. What a wonderful God we serve.

Our spirit makes us God-conscious. Our soul makes us self-conscious. Our body makes it possible for us to interact with the world in which we live. However, we believers in Christ are not to accept every supernatural spirit or activity that may appear.

We are instructed to be discerning, to pray and listen to the truth of things that are being said or done. They must agree with the Bible and the overall extensive character of our loving, just, and faithful God.

CHAPTER 10

Tammy and the Tall Slide

OUR ONLY daughter was a sweet, tiny girl. When Tammy was in the second grade, I had a wonderful experience regarding how God would protect her. I was reading the Psalms when a couple of verses really stood out! It was praise to the Lord for protection from injury from a fall. When quickened by the Holy Spirit and faith, holy scripture has the power to impart spiritual life and help us in various ways! (Romans 8:11)

It is alive, available, and active for believers. But how many really know that *the Word of God is spirit and life?* (John 6:63)

> *The Word of God is living and active, sharper than any two-edged sword... it can judge the thoughts and intentions of the heart.*
> HEBREWS 4:12, NRSV

God said that His Word *"shall not return unto me void, but it shall accomplish all that which I please, and it shall prosper in the thing whereto I sent it."* (Isaiah 55:11b KJV)

> *You have rescued me from death; you have kept my feet from slipping. So now I can walk in your presence, O God, in your life-giving light.*
> PSALM 56:13, NLT

Looking at these verses, I kept thinking of my little Tammy and that this promise was for her. I immediately began to pray on her behalf, declaring, "No! In Jesus' name, Tammy will not be hurt by falling!"

One day shortly after that, when I was picking her up from school, the teacher was standing beside her protectively. I wondered why. The teacher explained that Tammy had fallen off the tall slide on the playground but that she was fine—just a little frightened! I praised the Lord for her protection.

This exemplifies how the Lord uses His Word to help us. As Scripture says:

> *The Lord GOD has opened my ear, and I was not rebellious, neither turned away backward.*
> ISAIAH 50:5, NHEB

We need daily guidance that only the Lord can provide. Because the cares of life are so real, we dare not let them overpower His voice. We will be helped as we make it a point to discipline ourselves and give Him quality time.

My Son, If Sinners Entice You, Go Not with Them

In the 1970s, when my kids got a little older, we bought a fixer-upper home next to the school my younger children would attend. Craig, however, was going to be in a middle school that was considered rough, which made me nervous.

I wouldn't leave in the mornings without us praying over their day. One day a scripture rang in my ears, and I felt it was for Craig. I kept hearing this verse:

> *My son, if sinners lure you, do not go along!*
> PROVERBS 1:10, GW

With that upon me, as I was driving him to school, every minute or so, I would look over at him and repeat, *"My son, if sinners entice you, **do not** go along!"*

Well, after he grew up to college age, Craig said that on that day, he had planned to go with several kids who were going to skip school and go out running around. But after I obeyed the Holy Spirit and exhorted him all the way from the house to the school, he decided not to go with them.

We will not know until eternity what the Holy Spirit saved my son from that day. Oh, how I praise God that He is a Good Father. Jesus said, *"I am with you always."* (Matthew 28:20). Ephesians 1:3 says that God is *"the father of mercies and comfort."* We have not been left as orphans. (John 14:18)

> *As the heavens are higher than the earth, so are My ways higher than your ways, and My thoughts than your thoughts.*
> ISAIAH 55:9, NKJV

Aren't we glad, too, that His *ways* involve His *timing*? He also knows the best time to do it! Now we are facing unsettling times that feel menacing and deep.

Seeing Like God Sees: Craig and the Hot Oil

I am so glad that Jesus said, The Spirit of truth will show you things to come. He shall glorify me, for he will take of mine and show it to you."

> *All things that the Father has are mine: therefore I said that he shall take of mine, and shall show* it *to you.*
> JOHN 16:15, AKJV

We must understand that the overly busy routine of life can steal our quiet time and therefore steal His words from us. I see that the Holy Spirit often gives insight while in my prayer closet or garden. This is when my mind and spirit are quiet.

One day in that quiet spirit, I saw my oldest son Craig, who was in his teens then. He had a job at a fast-food place. He was carrying a pot of scalding oil. I saw him stumble, fall, and spill hot oil all over himself.

I began to pray and cry, "No! In the name of Jesus! This is not going to happen to my son. No!"

I continued to pray about this vision. That evening my doorbell rang, and there stood Craig with one of the workers from his job. There was a white cloth on his arm. They explained Craig had been carrying a pot of hot oil, then stumbled and fell.

We praised God all the way while driving him to the emergency room, thankful that his eyes and face weren't burned. The ER doctor put a little salve on the wound and told me to take him to his doctor the next day.

The following day we went to the doctor, but when we took the white cloth away, there was only a tiny red spot. I praised the Lord for the insight of the vision so that I could pray and stand for my son's safety.

The Bible records many instances of God-given visions. For example, Peter had a vision that would lead him to go and minister to the house of Cornelius. (Acts 10:9)

Aren't you glad that Jesus taught us about the work of the Holy Spirit? He said that "*when the spirit of truth has come, he will guide you into all truth; he will glorify me, for he will take what is mine and declare it to you!* " (John 16:13-14 NKJV para) The Holy Spirit is the Spirit of Jesus, our Standby, who awaits to teach, comfort, and help us when we do not know how to pray.

Yes. *He will show you things to come.* A deep quiet thankfulness swept over me every time I thought about it. How thankful I am yet today for that insight that took me to prayer, saving my son from devastating burns!

Yes, there is a God, and He so loved the world that He gave us Jesus, His Word, and the Holy Spirit. He does not leave us alone as orphans; we are His dear children, He provides what is needed throughout our life.

Baby Brent: Fear Defeated, Sickness healed!

Nothing is more precious to a mother than seeing her newborn child for the very first time! And that was the case when Brent, our blond-haired son, was born in 1969. As our last baby, he would complete our little family. When he was eight weeks old, the Holy Spirit began nudging me to spend more time in prayer. It was during this time that I had a very scary vivid dream.

In the dream, I was in a room alone, and the atmosphere became very dark and sinister. Gradually, the power went off and I became paralyzed. The door slowly shut and locked. A dark power filled the room.

At that point, I spoke one word in prayer: "JESUS!" As I did, everything gradually returned to normal. The power came back on. The heater and vaporizer came on. The door unlocked and opened.

When Brent was two months old, I discovered exactly why I had been given the vivid dream. We decided he was old enough to make the four-hour trip to Llano, in Central Texas, to show him off to the family. Frank loaded the baby bed into the car, and we gathered ten-year-old Craig and six-year-old Tammy, and off we went.

In Llano, I woke up so sick with the flu that I couldn't even raise my head off the pillow. My mother had left with Brent to show off her newest grandchild at a friend's shower, but she came home with the bad news that he was burning up with a fever. Frank took him to the doctor, who warned him that he would have to be hospitalized if his condition didn't improve. The diagnosis? *Salmonella.* Frank and I were devastated. Already very sick myself, this news only intensified my battle. I was consumed with fear.

But then I remembered the dream and realized the Holy Spirit had shown me things to come (John 16:13). He had given me that vision, so that despite the current crisis, I could be comforted and know everything would be okay. The fear vanished and I felt a fresh infusion of faith which gave me peace and comfort. Soon baby Brent was healed, and so was I.

CHAPTER 11

Life and Death

IT WAS A Saturday night in 2003. I was really struggling while preparing to teach our Sunday morning youth group. I felt my topic was way too heavy. After prayer though, I knew this message was from God. Here is the title of the teaching for our youth group, based on (Job 14:14): "LIFE and DEATH. Can the dead live again?" The Sunday morning news was of our astronauts' deaths!

My teaching points are still relevant today because we live in a chaotic and uncertain world! So, I will ask the question again: Can The Dead Live Again? (Job 14:14)

1. Scripture points out the brevity of life. It is appointed unto humanity once to die and then the judgment (Hebrews 9:27).
2. We must examine ourselves to be certain that we are in faith. (2 Peter 1:10, RSV)

Oh, the sweet assurance of our salvation through Jesus' death and resurrection! Blessed be the Apostle John, who said:

> *I have written this to you who believe in the name of the Son of God, so that you may know you have eternal life.*
> 1 JOHN 5:13, NLT

So, I continued with this teaching flow:

1. Share the need for the Baptism in the Holy Spirit, so we can be empowered for a fruitful life, have the boldness to spread the good news of Jesus, and help one another (Acts 1-2).
2. Hold onto the promises of God and throw out any sense of guilt or condemnation that torments us.

> *There is therefore now no condemnation for those who are in Christ Jesus.*
> ROMANS 8:1, ESV

> *If we say that we have no sin, we deceive ourselves, and the truth is not in us. If we confess our sins, he is faithful and just to forgive us our sins, and to cleanse us from all unrighteousness.*
> 1 JOHN 1:8-9, AKJV

Safe in the Arms of Jesus

A woman who worked for us once a week was a single mother with a 16-year-old son named George. She was heavy-hearted because he was hanging out with a rebellious crowd. God led me to pray for them, and in about a week, He gave me a plan.

I sent word to George that if he attended the upcoming church camp, I would cover all his expenses and buy him new clothes. After a week, he accepted my offer. So, I met him and bought his new clothes. He went to camp, and there he gave his life to Jesus!

Jesus had become real to him. When he got home from camp, he was testifying to all his friends. He told everyone who would listen! Two weeks later, he was killed in a drive-by shooting. Amid our grief and tears, we had a godly peace and comfort that Jesus had His beloved lost sheep.

> *"I am the resurrection and the life. Anyone who believes in Me will live, even after dying. Everyone who lives in Me and believes in Me will never ever die."*
> JOHN 11:25-26, NLT

George was like the lost sheep Jesus spoke of.

> *So he told them this parable: "Which one of you, having a hundred sheep and losing one of them, does not leave the ninety-nine in the wilderness and go after the one that is lost until he finds it? And when he has found it; he lays it on his shoulders and rejoices. And when he comes home, he calls together his friends and neighbors, saying to them, 'Rejoice with me, for I have found my lost sheep.' Just so, I tell you, there will be more joy in heaven over one sinner who repents than over ninety-nine righteous people who need no repentance."*
> LUKE 15:3-7, NRSVUE

His Sheep Am I

On our journey through life, it may, at times, seem we are alone. During those dark and difficult times, it is comforting to know God has promised never to leave us.

> *He [God] has said, "I will never [under any circumstances] desert you [nor give you up nor leave you without support, nor will I in any degree leave you helpless], nor will I forsake or let you down or relax My hold on you [assuredly not]!" So, we take comfort and are encouraged and confidently say, "The Lord is my Helper [in time of need], I will not be afraid.*
> HEBREWS 13:5-6, AMP

I was reminded of this a few years ago when we received care at a clinic in California, Frank was recovering from triple bypass heart surgery, and I was feeling distressed. My nerves were ragged, and I needed help being able to get some good sleep.

What gave me comfort during that time was our friend, Sally. I knew she was back home interceding for us. What a gift from God!

One day at the clinic, I had a vision that brought me deep peace. In the image, Jesus, our Shepherd, stood in the sunshine inside the sheepfold. He was relaxed as He watched over the sheep, and His eyes radiated love for them. The sheep had the same deep love in their eyes as they looked at their Shepherd. One sheep was leaning on Him. I knew it was me! Around my neck, I wore a gold bell on a red ribbon.

It was so clear to me that the Good Shepherd was caring for His sheep. They were settled, contented, and loved. It was twilight, so the sheep were in the fold for the night. There they would be safe. This gave me such peace and assurance! Amid uncertainties, we can rest in the fact that we are *never* alone. Our Shepherd is always with us.

I don't have the talent to draw or to paint the powerful vision, but it's etched forever in my Spirit. And I know that Jesus loves us so much. He cares for each of us as a good shepherd cares for his sheep. (Psalm 23)

Jesus, Himself said:

> *I am the good Shepherd. The good Shepherd risks*
> *and lays down His [own] life for the sheep.*
> JOHN 10:11, AMP

Like a good Shepherd, the LORD knows each one of us intimately, and we know His voice. We do well to frequently rehearse the fact that we are never alone! We are covered by His unfailing love. How wonderful that we can express that same love and comfort to one another. It may mean a note, a card, or a visit. It may mean calling for group prayer. The result is that we can give and receive the Lord's strength, comfort, and peace for one another.

I was thankful for a true friend like Sally. I experienced comfort, knowing she was concerned and was calling on the Lord on my behalf. I felt her prayers! And in my weak condition, it was like medicine.

She showed up at my door weeks later with a little white sheep she had created for me—and it had a gold bell on a ribbon around its neck! To this day, seeing this little sheep comforts me.

CHAPTER 12

The Value of Family Support

WHEN LIFE pulls the rug out from under us, and we are in the valley of despair, be sure that Jesus intercedes for us, praying that our faith won't fail.

> *Let your roots grow down into him*
> *and draw up nourishment from him.*
> COLOSSIANS 2:7, TLB

God gave my son Craig a simple word of wisdom: "Don't be foolish with your choices."

Every encounter here shows that God is supernatural and knows every detail of your life. He is the Almighty Father of mercies and comfort.

This faith is not natural, like our five senses of what we touch, taste, smell, hear, and see. Faith is listed as one of the spiritual gifts.

> *Faith is the substance of things hoped for, the*
> *evidence of things not seen.*
> HEBREWS 11:1, NKJV

The life of King David, from the Bible, often encouraged me. This mighty man of war was designated as a young child to be God's choice to reunify Israel and be crowned King. As he grew and faced impossible odds and led fierce battles, he said, *when I am afraid, I will put my trust in you, God.* (Psalm 56:3) In the end, though not a perfect man, he reunified his country and wore the Kingly crown!

We need faith, but it is also true that we need hope. In fact, apart from God, my case was hopeless. I needed hope! My hope was in the Lord because when medical science had no answer, He did!

During my seeking for my healing, God did something I thought was highly unusual. He spoke inside me repeatedly, saying, "Sing, Mary!"

I thought, *How can you ask this of me, Lord! The active life and ministry I had loved for so long is gone because I'm in so much pain.*

To my surprise, my youngest son Brent, *not knowing* what God had spoken to me, called to me from upstairs one day, "Mom, you always used to sing. You need to sing. Sing, Mom! Sing like you used to." How surprising and inspiring this was to me!

God knew that I needed to sing out words of love and faith to Him. Science reports *now* that the body responds to the brain's speech center. The church family long ago knew that scriptures caution us about the power of the tongue, for good or evil. God listens. I kept thinking of the hymn "His Eye is on the Sparrow."

At first, I could only whisper it. I found that a whisper in faith can change the atmosphere! In every ordeal, our faith-filled words can help to lift us. Reading about King David's tormenting trials after such victories was a help to me.

> *Why are you cast down, O my soul?*
> *And why are you disquieted within me?*
> *Hope in God; For I shall yet praise Him,*
> *The help of my countenance and my God.*

My family strengthened me with their continual prayers. Frank, my husband, often laying his hand on my body, continually spoke out strong prayers for healing.

Let us recall how Jesus taught that He came to bring life. He taught that it is the devil, the evil one, who comes to steal, kill, and destroy (John 10:10). So, the fact remains: God wants us to be well.

To help us, He provided several different avenues for us to recover wellness, and so I pressed in to receive my healing. I learned so much to share with others. And I took James' directive seriously when he wrote:

> *Are any of you sick? You should call for the elders*
> *of the church to come and pray over you,*
> *anointing you with oil in the name of the Lord.*
> *Such a prayer offered in faith will heal the sick,*
> *and the Lord will make you well. And if you have*
> *committed any sins, you will be forgiven.*
> JAMES 5:14-15, NLT

So, armed with this biblical truth, I went everywhere that I knew prayer was being offered. I needed to receive prayer for healing. After a while, I began to improve. I could feel my body was indeed healing!

Scripture tells us to be humble. *Cleanse ourselves of sin and of pride; resist the devil, and he will flee from you.* (James 4:6-8 NKJV para) Scripture tells us, too, that in our battles, we are armed with the Word of God and the Spirit of God.

The Word is *the sword of the Spirit* (Ephesians 6:17) and is quick, powerful, and sharper than any two-edged sword. (Hebrews 4:12)

The Holy Spirit, who comes to our aid and helps us to pray when we don't know how, was urging me on. Armed with Truth, I chose to believe the fact that I was healed, and I was waiting for it to manifest!

The day finally came when all the symptoms were gone. I arose to serve the Lord again with a new faith. I now had a greater insight into the good fight of faith. Scriptures like Romans 8:32 had come alive!

> *Since he did not spare even his own Son but gave*
> *him up for us all, won't he also*
> *give us everything else?*
> ROMANS 8:32, NLT

Christ Jesus died and was raised to life for us. He is sitting in the place of honor and authority at God's right hand, interceding for us (Matthew 26:64; Romans 8:34; and Hebrews 4-10).

But what about when trouble comes? Does it mean He no longer loves us if we experience trouble and tribulation? No! Not at all.

> *It is Christ who died, and furthermore is also risen,*
> *who is even at the right hand of God, who also*
> *makes intercession for us. Who shall separate us*
> *from the love of Christ? Shall tribulation, or distress,*
> *or persecution, or famine, or nakedness, or peril, or*
> *sword?... Yet in all these things we are more than*
> *conquerors through Him who loved us. For I am*
> *persuaded that neither death nor life, nor angels nor*
> *principalities nor powers, nor things present nor*
> *things to come, nor height nor depth, nor any other*
> *created thing, shall be able to separate us from the*
> *love of God which is in Christ Jesus our Lord.*
> ROMANS 8:34-39, NKJV

Indeed, in all these things, overwhelming victory is ours through Christ, who loves us.

God Gives us Beauty for Ashes

Although I have already shared about my healing from fibromyalgia, I want to share more to help anyone needing extra help and inspiration. I began losing my health and living in relentless pain, but doctors had difficulty diagnosing it. It was new in those early days, so it was a while before we knew what it was. How depressing when I learned there was no cure. I was sick for around ten years. Thank God, I began receiving the manifestation of divine healing progressively in the year of 2004 and was healed by 2005.

The reality was that I was sick, and there was no cure. My active life with family and the ministry was gone. Long years of fibromyalgia—with its pain, chronic fatigue, brain fog, depression, and isolation—had plunged me into deep despair. Still, I found much comfort in David's cry for help.

> *My soul is cast down within me. By day the Lord commands his steadfast love, and at night his song is with me, a prayer to the God of my life. I say to God, my rock, "Why have you forgotten me? Why must I walk about mournfully because the enemy oppresses me?" Why are you cast down, O my soul, and why are you disquieted within me? Hope in God; for I shall again praise him, my help and my God.*
> PSALM 42:1-11, NRSV

David poured out the deep despair of his heart, yet I saw how he sprinkled the Psalm with some amazing statements of determined hope and faith! He declares, "*I will again praise my Savior and my God!*" This felt good. He gives us this wonderful example of how we can honor God and speak of our faith in Him in the worst of times.

He also shows the power of faith-filled words to lift us. We all face struggles, and with God's help, we must share how the Lord has healed, helped us, or sustained us through hard times. By doing this, our testimony honors Him and encourages others in their time of need.

An Astonished French Tour Guide

In 2008, Frank and I were vacationing in France. One day, we took a break from touring and were outdoors enjoying lunch. Suddenly, I received one of the Holy Spirit's spiritual gifts, the word of knowledge, which is knowledge we have no earthly way of knowing.

The word of knowledge I had heard was simply, "She was raised on a farm." This was a spiritual gift sent to tell me that our tour guide was raised on a farm so that I could repeat this to her.

The LORD had a desire that she could know He is real and that He cared about her. It was simple, but I could see by her reaction that it was very impacting. I had not met her before the tours. She knew we were strangers.

When I simply said, "You were raised on a farm," her eyes grew wide, and she leaned toward me with a puzzled look of great astonishment. I saw her entire demeanor change in an instant. She exclaimed, "I did not tell you that!"

It was plain to see that she did not know how this could possibly be that a stranger on vacation, suddenly out of the blue, could speak of such a personal time in her life in such a matter-of-fact way! This seemed most certainly something she had never encountered before. She asked again, "How did you know that?"

I was happy to say, "This has come from our Lord Jesus by His Holy Spirit's gifts. He wants you to come close, give yourself to Him and know He loves you."

He was drawing her with "cords of love" to Himself. She became very soft in her facial features. What Holy ground! That night I packed to leave, but oh, I wanted to tell her more of the glories of our gracious Almighty God.

I sat down and wrote her a long letter about our loving Savior and left it in the care of the hotel desk clerk. Dear LORD Jesus, how can I thank you for allowing me to be part of this beautiful, incredible divine encounter!

CHAPTER 13

Women's Aglow Encounters

IN FEBRUARY 2009, I ministered at the Aglow Chapter in Katy, Texas. I was happy to meet Jan, the Chapter President. As I laid hands on each leader and prayed, the Lord met us. In meetings like this, I will share my testimony of healing from fibromyalgia and speak about the gifts of healing. I think the entire room came for prayer, again showing the great need for one another's prayers.

We need our elders laying on of hands, as well as our brothers and sisters' prayers. During this time of personal ministry, God gave words of knowledge for each woman. As a result, each one was encouraged, comforted, assured, and strengthened.

After the meeting, the leader introduced me to Pastor George, in whose church we were meeting. He and I prayed for each other and prophesied to me, "You have many long years of experience in the Spirit and the things of God. You minister effectively from that storehouse. But now you have come through many difficult, gloomy, dark seasons. Your habit is to spend much time in prayer, but you have hit smack against a brick wall in your prayers now."

It was true. Pastor George prayed encouragement for me and rebuked the enemy and the wall of deep despair I was dealing with. He was right! I had been struggling. We all must push through some hard times. This sensitive pastor gave me the fresh hope and renewed strength I needed.

Faithful is He Who Calls You, Who Also Will Do It

I was scheduled to minister at the Aglow Meeting in Alvin, Texas, where I would teach about healing and pray for healing. God is a healer and Jesus moved in great compassion and healed the sick among them in His day. Without faith, we cannot please God, but according to the Bible, we have each been given a measure of faith from Him. God freely gives us words of life and spiritual gifts.

On the day of the meeting, Donna Tully, a good friend, called me. She was excited because that day, while in the spirit, she saw me teaching on the Gifts of the Holy Spirit, and many people were receiving what they heard and then passing it on to others. I was stunned because she had no way of knowing what I was doing or where I was going that day! God is an encourager!

I had a speaking engagement that evening at the Aglow Chapter in the NASA area of Houston. It was a dark, drizzly night. What a trial it was getting there! The unfamiliar territory and construction detours caused me to go in circles, wasting time. I could not miss this meeting! But truly:

> *But we have this treasure in earthen vessels, that*
> *the excellency of the power may be of God,*
> *and not of us.*
> 2 CORINTHIANS 4:7, NKJV

I had a mandate to teach the Gifts of Healing and to pray healing over the women. I didn't feel strong and sure that night! Finally, I arrived—a complete ball of nerves—as the group finished dinner. As I began teaching, an amazing total calm and clear focus fell on me so I could minister effectively to my sisters.

At that NASA meeting, a woman received prayer for healing from fibromyalgia, and the following week she reported she was healed. Another was relieved of long-term shoulder pain. I also prayed for a woman who had a need for transportation. Shortly after that meeting, she received a vehicle. God met her needs. He wants to fill us all with His spirit so that we can help one another. If we give ourselves to Him, He will empower us.

How happy are those whose strength comes from God! What a holy honor to be used by Him.

> *God promises to console those who mourn in Zion, to give them beauty for ashes, the oil of joy for mourning, the garment of praise for the spirit of heaviness that they may be called trees of righteousness, the planting of the Lord, that He may be glorified.*
> ISAIAH 61:3, NKJV

> *But He was wounded for our transgressions, He was bruised for our iniquities; the chastisement for our peace was upon Him, and by His stripes we are healed.*
> ISAIAH 53:5, NKJV

Encouragement

> *If your gift is to encourage others, be encouraging. If it is giving, give generously. If God has given you leadership ability, take the responsibility seriously. If your gift is in showing kindness to others, do it gladly.*
> ROMANS 12:8, NLT

In 2013, I was a scheduled speaker at the Southeast Texas Aglow Conference in Stafford, Texas. When I woke up at 3:15 AM the night before, I thought, *No way!* I wanted to feel strong and energetic to teach and tell my healing testimony. My entire body felt so exhausted I could hardly think! I needed strength for the in-depth healing teaching I planned to present. I reminded myself how God pours Himself into us, empowering our earthen vessels through His grace and mercy. Christ, in us, is the Treasure in our earthen vessel.

Frank came to support me. As I shared my healing from fibromyalgia, he was teary-eyed, recalling how long he prayed continuously for me and lived through those terrible years of sickness with me. But then he also was an eyewitness to the great miracle of my healing! The long line of people coming for prayer after my testimony showed the tremendous need for healing.

God empowered me to minister to the needy ones. The encouragement coming to me from the leaders was a special blessing! I was scheduled to speak following Carol Torrance, who was a well-known, much-loved minister, as well as a Director of Aglow U.S. Regional. With a glad heart, I received a note from my beloved Cathy Campbell, President of the Aglow Chapter in Sugar Land, Texas, for years. She called my message "power-packed." We well knew that power flows from the Living Word of God!

Biblically, encouraging one another is an activity that we all need and is well pleasing to our Lord. Carolynn Connelly, beloved President of the River Oaks Texas Aglow Chapter for years, reached out to me. I treasured her comments, along with a note I received from our friend, Donice Walker. The message of God's love, mercy, and healing is wonderful! What a joy it is to encourage others, but also it is strengthening to be encouraged ourselves.

A Miracle Bridge to Europe

In the fall of 2006, I was participating in a time of intercession that was meeting in Branson, Missouri. During a season of prayer, I felt the Lord's Army, a contingent of soldiers of the Cross was being sent to London to carry out God's plans and purpose. I saw these men and women arriving over bridges that had been created purely by intercessors in prayer.

Directing this operation was the Creator of the Universe, who longed for London to turn to Him. And because of His great love, He would take action to pour out His blessing upon that great city. This was my first experience in interceding for nations and places. And never had I prayed like this for London or Europe. God was having me pray and, over the next few years, calling out for Europe's help in intercession.

During this season, I had a vision that involved Pastor Lenny Weston, a friend, and the founder of *Vision Ministries* in Ohio, later called The Bridge Church. In the vision, I saw Pastor going into Europe over a single bridge, and so I decided to pray for the bridge that God had for him to enter that continent. I was familiar with

SURPRISED BY THE SPIRIT - 121

Pastor Lenny's ventures because I was hosting a weekly prayer group in my home for his ministry.

Our focus was *The Timothy Project,* the youth mission's ministry he founded. It is hard to describe the love of God for the youth. Intense prayers and spiritual gifts were experienced in those small meetings! How we need the power of prayer for our young adults today.

I knew the Holy Spirit was creating the bridge to take the Gospel into Europe, but also I kept hearing *Sunderland.* That seemed like a funny word. I asked around about it, but no one knew what it meant. During the four or five months of these weekly prayer meetings, I had not spoken much with the ministry office. Then one day, the office in Columbus, Ohio, called. They were so excited, saying they had received an amazing call from *The God Channel* (television) in Europe! They asked for permission to televise *Vision Ministry's* videos throughout Europe, free of charge.

How astonished we were to learn that the email confirming the request came from Sunderland, England! Finally, we learned Sunderland was the center of the great *Pentecostal Revival* in England. Alexander Boddy (1854–1930), one of the founders of Pentecostalism in Britain, was the rector of All Saints Church of England, serving in an area of Sunderland! There, on October 28, 1907, the famous evangelist Smith Wigglesworth was baptized in the Holy Spirit of God.

This knowledge was an encouragement that wherever Lenny Weston found himself, the Holy Spirit would reach out to bring souls to our gracious LORD.

Many lives were impacted through Pastor Lenny Weston and the faithful who ministered with him. I was privileged to minister in a powerful weekend retreat for the women there.

I could hardly believe that I was also asked to preach the first Sunday service ever at the church, which they founded in Columbus, Ohio.

Here I was in Texas, but I loved and felt close to this whole incredibly dedicated group. What an extreme blessing that I was still having a part in it. Our dearly loved Pastor Lenny went to his eternal reward in 2019.

CHAPTER 14

Mississippi Surprise

FOR ONE of our vacations, Frank and I took a tour of the Mississippi River Delta. This is a very interesting historical region of our nation with a rich musical heritage. In fact, it is the birthplace of Blues and Gospel Music. One of the first places our guide took us was Commerce Boulevard Christian Church in Tunica, Mississippi. Pastor Evelyn Hubbard is an outstanding pastor but also a talented and well-known singer.

As the tour was ending, Pastor Hubbard thanked the tour group for visiting. I lifted my hand and waved to get her attention, and asked, "Are you going to send us away without letting us hear you sing?" You see, we had heard much information, but not all were touched spiritually yet. I thought there were people on that bus who needed the Lord's caring touch!

She hesitated. "I don't have a soundtrack," she said.

Very politely, I responded, "All you need is a microphone and the Lord."

And with that, she smiled and began to sing. Pastor Evelyn Hubbard sang a hymn with such anointing that it caused that little church to be filled with the palpable presence of the Lord! When she finished, we boarded the bus and were on our way.

As we traveled, one by one, almost everyone in the group came to me and very sincerely thanked me. Seeing God touching souls is the burning desire in my heart, but when I miss those precious prayer times with Him, life gets to be all about my concerns instead of about Him and others. Then I become hesitant, and I feel almost too vulnerable to reach out.

Looking at my fellow travelers, I knew God saw every heart. That is why He moved me to speak up and open the way for Him to comfort each one. Jesus is compassionate.

> *When He saw the multitudes, He was moved with compassion for them, because they were weary and scattered, like sheep having no shepherd.*
> MATTHEW 9:36, NKJV

In these situations, one way that we know His leading is that we sense a deep compassion at that moment in time. It reminds me of how Jesus was led by this compassion for people.

What an awesome life this is! I have times when I need to recall how God *gives us power to reach out.* (Acts 1:8,

NKJV para) God gives us the ability to see divine encounters that are unforgettable and encourages us today. *Fear not, little flock.* (Luke 12:32) *God's love has been poured into our hearts through the Holy Spirit that has been given to us.* (Romans 5:5, NRSV)

The Parking Lot Was Holy Ground

One day, after shopping for groceries, one of the workers—a young girl—carried my groceries to my car. Suddenly, I had a sense that she was hungry for God. This awareness came from the Holy Spirit. I asked, "Do you mind if I ask you a question?"

When she agreed, I asked about her spiritual life. I asked her if she knew if she would go to Heaven if she were to die that very night. When she said she was not, I told her about God's love for her and God's gift of eternal life in Heaven. I asked if she would like to give her life to Jesus. She agreed, and we prayed. She was so joyful; she hugged me and then told me her story.

She explained that lately, all her thoughts were consumed with wanting to be in church and raise her baby in church but was ashamed to go because she wasn't married. She felt that God would not forgive her or accept her. At that moment, His love and grace became real to her, and she was set free. She had a Bible, and I told her where to begin reading. What a huge blessing. This ability to help someone else isn't something we do in our own strength.

God gives us the gift of the Holy Spirit and the gifts of the Spirit to comfort and guide us personally so that He can work through us to help others. As Paul said, "*A spiritual gift is given to each of us so we can help each other.*" (1 Corinthians 12:7, NLT) God helps us learn to recognize and flow in the gifts. As we go along in life, we must learn to listen for His Voice. *God is love;* (1 John 4:8)

One very important thing to remember is that each assignment comes with a deep sense of compassion. I have found it a must start each day in a quiet place so the daily cares of life can't rob me of hearing the precious Holy Spirit.

A Spirit-Led Vision to Help Bryan

I woke up early one morning in the fall of 2014 seeing a picture of an odd shape. I did not understand what I was seeing. I decided to pray in my prayer language, and this brought comfort because I knew the Holy Spirit would let me know whatever I needed to know in His time. My mind didn't know what the Spirit was praying, but God did!

Soon, an idea came to me. I drew the oddly shaped picture I had seen, and I faxed it to our granddaughter, who is a nurse. I asked, "Could this be an aneurysm?"

"Yes!" She said.

Later in the day, I received a note from my friend Priscilla Jurena asking for prayer for friends, Memery and Bryan Hughes. She said that Bryan was suffering with an aneurysm and needed prayer. Finally, the pieces were fitting together, and I realized that I was praying for Bryan! He recovered well.

This experience illustrates one way that the Holy Spirit, who has come to live in us, communicates with us to help us. Sometimes, His direction is like what the Bible refers to as *a still, small voice.* (1 Kings 19:11-13)

One day I didn't listen to *that still, small voice* and wished that I had! I was drawing my bath but needed to get something from another room. As I turned to go to the other room, I heard, "Don't leave this room with the water running." I thought *it is okay*! Ten minutes passed before I remembered that the water was running! Panicked, I ran across the slippery floor, immediately slipped, and hit my head hard on the stone floor!

I learned an important lesson that day. God mercifully wanted me to avoid trouble. I recalled how Paul called God *the Father of our Lord Jesus Christ, and our Father, the Father of mercies and comfort.* Many in this world don't know the blessing of a merciful father. When humans cannot fill the role of father, the hurts they impart are products of their deep human brokenness. Jesus called God "Our Father." Only He can mend our broken relationships.

An Encounter, Rebuke a Spirit of Death

My husband and I decided to go to Austin to visit our daughter Tammy, her husband Blake, and their two little girls. We invited our teenage granddaughter, Amanda, and took her with us. Blake was at a men's retreat that weekend. Soon we were playing with our grandchildren and enjoying visiting with Tammy. Then there was a strange suggestion repeating in my thoughts. I heard, "Go into Blake's office and look at his books." I thought, *why would I be thinking that?*

I soon concluded that even though I couldn't understand this, it was the Holy Spirit guiding me. I went to Blake's office to scan the wall of bookshelves, and one book grabbed my attention. It was a book by Derek Prince, a very spiritual man of God who taught the Body of Christ. I opened it randomly, and my eyes fell on the title *How to Rebuke a Spirit of Death*. I read the page, reflected on it, closed the book, and went back to the family.

Later that day, Amanda got a frantic call from her Aunt Martha with the heartrending news that Amanda's mom, Elaine, had suffered a massive life-threatening stroke. Her doctors were calling in the family, saying they did not know if she would live through the night. Immediately, I recalled the earlier leading to the book, where I read about how to rebuke a spirit of death.

I was incredulous but thankful to know the Holy Spirit was clearly leading. He had let us know assuredly that Elaine had work to do, and this was not her time to go.

Blake and the men at the retreat were all praying. I began to pray and praise God for his mighty healing power working in Elaine's body. And for the power of knowing that his perfect will was for Elaine to live! We grabbed our bags. Frank drove Amanda in her car. I drove our car. This gave me three hours to pray in the Spirit and make faith proclamations for Elaine's life.

Amanda and I drove to the hospital, and when we finally found the ICU, Aunt Martha was sitting at her bedside. She told us Elaine was in a coma and that her right side was paralyzed. She had gone through extensive surgeries, and they had put in some stents in her brain. I loved Elaine. It was hard to see her all wired up.

Amanda and Aunt Martha talked as I stood at the foot of the bed with my hand on Elaine's right foot, praying in the Spirit. I was silently roaring, calling on God's power, and rebuking a spirit of death.

In less than five minutes, her foot began to twitch under my hand, and then her leg began to move. It was incredible to experience this and how seeing *a miracle under my hand seemed so natural.*

Next, I went up to the head of the bed and laid my hand on Elaine's arm, praying silently, but boldly inside using Jesus' name and authority. Seeing her arm begin to move, I stood in amazement. Amanda and I could go home and get some sleep.

A few days later, I went again to the ICU but Elaine Scantlin was not there. I learned she had been moved up to the third floor, so I went up to the third floor and saw an incredible sight: I found Elaine propped up in bed, all wires gone. She was laughing and talking with three or four friends who had brought flowers to cheer her up. What an incredible, unforgettable encounter. Lord, help us to listen for your Spirit's voice!

Today Elaine is happy. She totally lives to serve her Savior and needy souls. She is always ready to help and has a church family she dearly loves. Thank you, Almighty God, for sending the Holy Spirit to help and guide us. What a wonderful God you are! You do wondrous things!

A Tribute to Our Godly Grandmothers

Frank and I were aboard a small ship cruising the East Coast when one morning, I sensed the Spirit reaching for our young cabin keeper. I felt moved to write a full-page letter to her about God's great love for her.

When I saw her again, she melted into tears, and I did too! She said she had left a past behind and was now looking for a fresh new start—and this letter spoke personally to her!

Her cabin mate, surprisingly, also received the letter saying that it perfectly fit her life as well! They said they cried together and taped it up on their wall. Soon I learned that her godly grandmother, who was with the Lord now, had been a minister and a great influence.

I felt she had prayed much and given the children much support. I could almost see her prayers circling God's altar—circling there for this divine encounter!

Thank God for all the many grandmothers who have given up the freedoms of their personal life to raise and guide their grandchildren to a meaningful life with our Lord and Savior! I will never forget my time on that riverboat. I have grandchildren I cherish and pray over; I want to see them all close to Jesus as young as possible!

What a strong divine encounter. I look forward to praising God with these two women and that dear grandmother. What a rejoicing in Heaven one day.

CHAPTER 15

Amazing Encounter for Donna

DONNA WAS my coworker and secretary at Grace Assembly School of the Bible in Alief, Texas. She helped with the Bible school I helped to establish and where I served both as a teacher and administrator.

One day, when we were catching up on office work, it was obvious that Donna was having trouble breathing normally. She said it was a withdrawal from nicotine. As we returned to our work, I felt a powerful surge within. *It came with what I can only describe as holy love.*

As we worked, it was a distraction, and I sensed that the Holy Spirit was asking me how long we were going to tolerate this awful burden. He wanted us to deal with it then and there! Immediately I turned to her, laid my hand on her chest, and commanded that addicting, tormenting spirit to leave. I was in shock, realizing my hand felt like a strong vacuum cleaner pulling something up and out of her. We both felt it and described it the same way! Not only did her breathing become normal, but her whole body became quiet, and peace filled her being.

I stood totally speechless, with a holy fear and complete awe, Truly, our God exceeds our ability to describe. He rules the universe that He created. He is supernatural! The All-Powerful One. This flowing of the word of salvation and infilling of the blessed Holy Spirit is how we reach the world with God's love. This is how we live, love, train disciples, and help each other in the body of Christ! Today, how grateful we are for gifts of divine encounters!

Straw Doesn't Pass the Burn Test

During a special Christmas season, I was sitting in my church's Sunday morning service, feeling happy. Soon I was distracted. For no reason, my attention was continuously drawn to one of our leaders, who sat a few pews ahead of me. I didn't know him well, but he seemed like a good man.

Soon after, the Holy Spirit gave me a vision. I saw what looked like a 2x4 piece of wood going up his spine. It stopped just under the back of his head, and it seemed to be strong, sturdy, and totally immovable. Then, there also, I saw a bunch of straw. I was so puzzled and perplexed but got no immediate understanding.

I thought about baby Jesus being in a straw-filled manger, but that didn't seem right. When we see things not clearly understandable, it usually signals a need to go into serious prayer so that we perceive God's purpose. It will then be carried out as He wishes. Church ended, and I went home, totally engrossed with the vision. I began to pray and to ask God for clear understanding. Finally, I received insight that the 2x4 board represented a very rigid backbone and that, in turn, represented a rigid way of thinking.

I knew I was seeing him as God was seeing him. The Lord saw him as a very good man, a man who highly valued right from wrong. He would have every decision he made line up with doing the right thing as he saw it. I knew that the Holy Spirit recognized the man's good and honorable intentions, as well as his integrity.

Then I heard these words inside me: But he is so right, he is wrong! What an interesting thought! The Holy Spirit was saying that because the man was so rigid in his thinking, he found it hard to work well with others who held opinions different from his own.

My assignment was to tell him all I had been shown. As I continued to think about this, I remembered a Scripture about wood, hay, and stubble from the first letter that Paul wrote to the Corinthians.

No other foundation can anyone lay than that which is laid, which is Jesus Christ. Now if anyone builds on this foundation with gold, silver, precious stones, wood, hay, or straw, each one's work will become clear; for the Day will declare it because it will be revealed by fire; and the fire will test each one's work, of what sort it is. (1 Corinthians 3:11-13)

I knew that this man loved the Lord and earnestly served the Lord with all his heart, but that he would see many of his works burned up unless he could learn to have a more patient and humbler attitude and to work together with others. It was so clear that he loved the Lord, but he needed to see how harmful his rigid mindset was.

I respected this man and was very reluctant to do this, but I was aware that God was trusting me to do it. So, I called the pastor and asked to meet with him and his wife. As I began to lay out what I was so distressed about, they started laughing. I looked at them in disbelief because I didn't see anything funny about the situation.

The pastor said, "Oh, Mary! This man is a good man, but he has wrecked our business meetings. In fact, he has been such a problem that we've all been stressed out. I was so worn out trying to deal with him that I was beginning to wonder if he was born again!" Then he said they were worried about his soul's salvation.

I asked what they thought we should do, and they replied: "Mary, obey the Holy Spirit. We would like you to phone him. Tell him that you met with us and that we bear witness with your message, and that we believe this is a message from Our Lord."

I left the meeting feeling very much on the spot! I didn't know this man well and didn't know how he would respond to all this. But I was praying that God would help me so he could sense that this was truly of the Lord's direction. I was ready to make the call.

I related the whole story and honored the fact that he wanted to do what was right but that he needed to change in the ways that God was now directing. To my relief and surprise, he was receptive and confirmed what I had shared. He was ready to start following the Lord as he was being directed. Praise to the Lord.

> *Blessed be the LORD God, the God of Israel, who alone does wondrous things.*
> PSALM 72:18, NKJV

How our Lord loves and cares for each of us! He knows how to correct us without injuring us. As I thought about all this, I was so grateful.

The Winds of God at Stafford High

I was preparing to teach a Bible study for the small Christian youth club at Stafford High School in Stafford, Texas. Douglas Miner, the student who had founded the Christian Club and who attended the church that I attended, asked me to teach on the baptism of the Holy Spirit because he knew that his fellow classmates needed God's power to deal with their trials and troubles.

The day before I was to go to this school, I awoke while still under the lingering effect of a vivid dream in which two people were praying for me. The first person prayed sincerely. I appreciated it. But when the second person touched me, a power went through me. It seemed as if Heaven and Earth collided; and in a split second, I felt renewed in His presence!

I felt He was saying, "I have compassion for the children and the youth. I want to reach them, touch them, and fill them with a power for this age that will be life-changing. Hold back nothing, go teach, spread my love, be my voice, be my hands."

Later that day, I was scheduled to pray with friends. I was eager to share it all with them! When I began to share, I felt overcome with the weighty presence of the Lord. Our elders at church called this *The Shekinah Glory*. I felt very humble and amazed. I was being prepared to teach and pray for Douglas's High School Club! God treasures His youth and wants them to come quickly to Him.

The next day, I stood in front of the small group. I felt Jesus' love and saw weariness on many. After I taught the Bible truth of the Holy Spirit, I encouraged them to stay behind and seek to be Holy Spirit baptized. Those who stayed behind yielded themselves to God in prayer;

and as I prayed, God began to pour out His joy and refreshing. There is no joy like Joy in Jesus!

I recalled these scriptures:

> *But the Holy Spirit produces this kind of fruit in our lives: love, joy, peace....*
> GALATIANS 5:22A, NLT

> *For the kingdom of God is not eating and drinking, but righteousness and peace and joy in the Holy Spirit.*
> ROMANS 14:17, NKJV

For the next fifteen or twenty minutes, they laughed, cried, and walked through the room, speaking fluently in their new spiritual language. I've never seen such before or since. They were so joyful they grew louder and then two teachers knocked on the door to investigate. Douglas, in his gentle, matter-of-fact manner explained, "They are worshipping God, speaking in tongues."

They left but told him to keep the door open. I felt so much respect for this young man of God. Now, their faces seemed bright with joy and wonder! God rewarded Douglas' time and effort spent to establish this Bible study. May our young ones learn to give themselves to the great God of peace. Jesus said, "My Peace, I leave you. Let not your hearts be troubled."

I was so glad I was there when God did that! I will never forget the mighty love and joy they received during that Holy Spirit's outpouring.

A Baptism of Power

In 2020, I had the privilege of praying for Allison, a bright college-aged young woman. At the time, she had heard the CD of what I shared at the *Southeast Texas Aglow Conference*. My topic included "Walking in the Holy Spirit." She felt she was being drawn closer to God. She was moved and excited by my personal walk with the Holy Spirit and the spiritual gifts of the Spirit, and especially of the prophecy on CD that she had just listened to.

Soon I received an email in which she explained that she had committed herself to special missionary work. She said she was hungry to learn about the baptism in the Holy Spirit, and very eager to meet so I invited her to my home where we could investigate God's Word together. What a privilege to be able to teach and pray with such a hungry young woman! I knew that God was going to meet her.

God will guide young adults today to a strength that helps others also believe in His goodness and grace. I asked what had happened to cause her to seek the Lord so earnestly. She explained that the pandemic of 2020-2021 had caused her to evaluate her life as never before.

Then, one day in prayer, she experienced a call to serve the Lord in missions. I was impressed by her sincerity! As we talked, I shared many Scripture passages, and she listened intently. I wanted her to know the Bible, as God's word, was alive and powerful. God can speak to us personally, from its pages, for our unique situation, and at just the right time.

Then we looked at the passages on the coming of the Holy Spirit and His important roles as teacher, comforter, and guide, as well as the One who convicts our conscience when we need it and who helps us to pray when we do not know how. We looked at gifts of the Spirit, and she heard a good example of the gift of prophecy. She understood now that God wants to save souls, but also to baptize each one in the Holy Spirit, so God' gifts will flow in them.

As I shared, she followed along in her own Bible. I could see she longed to be discipled in the things of God. I was assured that she clearly understood all we had covered.

I said, "I can see that you have a good grasp of how the Holy Spirit leads; he will baptize you. When you are ready to receive prayer for the baptism in the Holy Spirit, let me know. I would count it a privilege to pray and lay hands on you."

She looked at me with excitement in her voice and said, "I want to pray now. I'm ready!"

So, I laid hands on her and prayed, "Receive the Holy Spirit."

What a sight to behold when she was suddenly filled with great joy! She smiled from ear to ear and shook her hands because, as she said, "They are all tingly. "

What a privilege and great joy to participate in her baptism! God loves and wants to guide and help our young adults to come and give themselves to Him.

The LORD Jesus Christ stands ready to empower our youth supernaturally in His word and grace so they will live in God-given righteousness. They will spread this Gospel of Peace from shore to shore.

We were both full of wonder, gratitude, and joy! Then off she went to share with her friends what she had learned and experienced freely from God's Holy Spirit. I knew she had stepped over into a new realm and would never ever be the same.

We see in scripture how both young and older people, who though they were filled with insecurity, fear, and doubt, were chosen by God for divine purposes, trained in faith and strengthened by God. They became leaders in divine interventions where God directed.

Many young leaders now are standing for God's purity and grace. They will reach out to the hurting with the promise that His grace is sufficient. The wonder and joy of encounters they see will help bring in God's harvest.

CONCLUSION

Wrapped in God's Unfailing Love

WE LIVE in a suffering, struggling, dark world. But through Jesus Christ, we are assured that our real citizenship is in Heaven, and we are urged not to forget all His benefits which we see in Psalm 103. The benefits of that truth are ours right now. The Psalmist said:

> *You, O Lord, are a shield for me, my glory and the One who lifts my head.*
> PSALM 3:3, NKJV

Through our trials, we pray in the Spirit, rejoice in our God-given Comforter, Helper, Stand by, and Guide, the One who prays the perfect prayers when we are so empty, tired, and feel at a loss for words. He is the one who helps us when all our strength is gone. We are His. He is ours!

You are of God, little children, and have overcome them, because He who is in you is greater than he who is in the world. (1 John 4:1) May all who read these encounters give themselves to God through the LORD Jesus and His mighty love.

ABOUT THE AUTHOR

MARY SCANTLIN is seasoned with years of experience as a Spirit-led leader and Bible teacher. Her passion has been participating with the Holy Spirit to impart help, hope, and faith to others through God's incredible, compassionate divine encounters. She longs to see others experience the Holy Spirit's encounters.

In 2005, Mary was freed from a prison of pain after a ten-year battle with fibromyalgia. She was also healed of other physical struggles and felt great empathy to encourage others. She has spearheaded and led various ministries and has been a frequent speaker for Aglow since 2004. In addition, she has conducted Bible studies in homes, churches, youth rallies, and a high school and ministered to a Bible study for women released from prison.

CONTACT INFORMATION

Mary Scantlin - Sugar Land, Texas

Mailing Address
13313 Redfish Lane, Suite 102
Stafford, TX 77477

Email: *divineencounters.info@gmail.com*

APPENDIX

Mary, after ministering at the *River Oaks Aglow Group*
meeting in Houston, Texas.

~ THE GOD OF PEACE ~

Jesus

WHO BROUGHT UP
JESUS FROM THE DEAD,
THE GREAT SHEPHERD OF THE SHEEP,
THROUGH THE ETERNAL BLOOD COVENANT,
~ EVEN JESUS OUR LORD ~
WILL MAKE YOU PERFECT IN EVERY GOOD WORK
TO DO HIS WILL, WORKING IN YOU
THAT WHICH IS PLEASING IN HIS SIGHT.
AS YOU FOLLOW AND LEARN OF HIM.

God IS Love

Jesus

GENTLE
Shepherd ~

Jesus said, "Whoever loves me will obey my
teaching. My Father will love them,
and my Father and I will come
and make our home within them.
Bible John 14:23

Jesus said ... Follow me Learn of me.

God IS Love

Mary and her husband, Frank Scantlin

Mary and her brother, Dale Fry

Elaine and Amanda Scantlin
(see Chapter 14)

Made in the USA
Middletown, DE
05 November 2023

41844930R00086